Scotland's leading educational publishers

MURPHY

Practice Papers for SQA Exams

National 5

History

D1388648

ISBN 9780007504985

Published by
Leckie & Leckie Ltd
An imprint of HarperCollins*Publishers*
Westerhill Road, Bishopbriggs, Glasgow, G64 2QT
T: 0844 576 8126   F: 0844 576 8131
leckieandleckie@harpercollins.co.uk   www.leckieandleckie.co.uk

Special thanks to
Jill Laidlaw (copy edit); Alistair Coats (proofread);
Ink Tank (cover design); QBS (layout)

Printed in Italy by Lego, S.P.A.

A CIP Catalogue record for this book is available from the British Library.

Acknowledgements

Exam A, Section 1, Part A, Source B:
About the crowning of Robert Bruce as King in 1306.
Adapted from A.D.M. Barrell, *Medieval Scotland*, 2000, Cambridge University Press

Exam A, Section 1, Part E, Source A:
Describes the use of tanks during the Battle of Cambrai 1917.
Adapted from *Britain at War 1914-1919*, Craig Mair, John Murray

Exam A, Section 2, Part A, Source A:
Written by Gerald of Wales about King Henry II.
Reprinted by permissionof HarperCollins Publishers Ltd © 2012 Daniel Jones

Exam A, Section 2, Part A, Source A:
Adapted from *An Illustrated History of the Crusades* by W.B Bartlett, The History Press

Exam A, Section 3, Part A, Source C:
Describes Richard I towards the end of the Third Crusade.
Adapted from *The Crusades*, Terry Jones and Alan Ereira, BBC Books. Reproduced by permission of Random House

Exam A, Section 3, Part D, Source A:
The impact of the Great Depression on German politics.
Adapted from Spartacus Educational website:
http://www.spartacus.schoolnet.co.uk/GERunemployment.htm

Exam A, Section 3, Part D, Source B:
The impact of the Great Depression on German politics.
Adapted from *Nazi Germany*, Stephen Lee, Pearson Education Limited

Exam B, Section 1, Part B, Source A:
About the consequences of the Rough Wooing.
Adapted from *Scotland: A New History*, Michael Lynch, Pimlico. Reproduced courtesy of Penguin Random House

Exam B, Section 1, Part B, Source B:
Message from Mary to Elizabeth
Reprinted by permission of HarperCollins Publishers Ltd © 2004 John Guy

Exam B, Section 1, Part D, Source A:
About migration from the Highlands and Lowlands of Scotland in the 19th Century
Adapted from *Scottish Emigration: Going for Good* by Roger Hudson. History Today Volume: 62 Issue: 6 2012 (http://www.historytoday.com/roger-hudson/scottish-emigration-going-good)

Exam B, Section 1, Part D, Source B:
Account of Irish sugar-workers in Greenock, 1836 from a Report on the State of the Irish Poor in Great Britain, Parliamentary Papers.
Adapted from Ireland in Schools website:
http://www.iisresource.org/Documents/Irish_In_Britain_Booklet_02.pdf

Exam B, Section 3, Part B, Source A:
Describes the Tsar's government of Russia between 1905 and 1914.
Adapted from Heinemann *Scottish History for Standard Grade: Russia 1914-41*, Colin Bagnall, Pearson Education Limited

Exam B, Section 3, Part B, Source B:
Describes the Tsar's government of Russia between 1905 and 1914.
Adapted from *Russia under the Bolshevik Regime*, Richard Pipes, Alfred Knopf Inc. Reproduced by permission of Random House

Exam B, Section 3, Part H, Source A:
About the Treaty of Versailles signed in June 1918
Adapted from the History Learning Site:
http://www.historylearningsite.co.uk/treaty_of_versailles.htm

Exam B, Section 3, Part H, Source B:
About the reasons why Britain adopted a policy of Appeasement towards Germany in the 1930s.
Adapted from BBC Bitesize website: http://www.bbc.co.uk/bitesize/higher/history/roadwar/appease/revision/2/

Exam C, Section 1, Part C, Source A:
About the Worcester Affair
Crown copyright: National Records of Scotland, A Union for a' That DVD (2007)

Exam C, Section 2, Part C, Source A:
Court Records from Dominica
Adapted from the National Archives website: http://www.nationalarchives.gov.uk/education/lessons/2388-popup.htm

Exam C, Section 3, Part G, Source B:
About immigration into America
Adapted from Shmoop: http://www.shmoop.com/1920s/immigration.html

Exam C, Section 3, Part I, Source A:
About the Japanese attack on Pearl Harbour in November 1941
Adapted from the BBC History Website: http://www.bbc.co.uk/history/worldwars/wwtwo/pearl_harbour_01.shtml

Exam C, Section 3, Part I, Source B:
About the Japanese attack on Pearl Harbour in November 1941
©2013 Jennifer Rosenberg (http://history1900s.about.com/). Used with permission of About Inc., which can be found online at www.about.com. All rights reserved

Exam C, Section 3, Part I, Source C:
About the Nazi occupied Europe
Adapted from *The Second World War* (Heinemann History), Nigel Kelly, Pearson Education Limited

Exam D, Section 1, Part A, Source A:
About the Scottish uprising against Edward in 1297
Adapted from *Scotland: A New History*, Michael Lynch, Pimlico. Reproduced courtesy of Penguin Random House

Exam D, Section 1, Part C, Source A:
Discusses the reasons for the introduction of the Treaty of Union.
Adapted from *Scotland: A New History*, Michael Lynch, Pimlico. Reproduced courtesy of Penguin Random House

Exam D, Section 1, Part C, Source B:
From a letter written by the Earl of Mar to the Earl of Oxford in 1711
National Records of Scotland, GD124/15/1024/12

Exam D, Section 3, Part F, Source A:
About Mussolini's domestic policies.
Reprinted by permission of HarperCollins Publishers Ltd © 2008 Derrick Murphy and Terry Morris

Exam D, Section 3, Part F, Source C:
About the Abyssinian crisis of 1935-6.
Adapted from *An Illustrated History of Modern Europe 1789-1984*, Denis Richards, Pearson Education Limited

Exam D, Section 3, Part J, Source B:
About the building of the Berlin Wall in 1961.
Adapted from *The Oxford Illustrated History of Modern Europe* edited by Blanning (2000). Reproduced by permission of Oxford University Press

Introduction

The best reason of all for studying history is because it is full of interesting stories, fascinating people, and strange and different worlds in which people did things differently to today. Hopefully, via history, you have learned a lot about what the world is like and how things have come to be the way they are. Above all I hope you have had fun with the past. However, now you are getting ready for your first major examination – you need to get in training!

An athlete will prepare for a specific event in a major championship by practising the skills that are relevant to their event. You should take every opportunity to rehearse the skills that you will need in the examination that forms the major part of the 'value added' element of the National 5 course. Some of these skills will overlap with the skills that you use in your assignment. For example, you need to know specific facts about your chosen topic; you need to organise those facts into an explanation, picking out the most important ones; you need to write all of that down in sentences that make sense on their own and all together. All of these skills will stand you in good stead in the examination.

However, just as a sprinter would want to copy exactly the conditions under which they would run the 100 metres when preparing for the Olympics or Commonwealth Games, you should, as much as possible, attempt examination questions of the type that you will face in the summer. A sprinter would not train by running the marathon or playing golf!

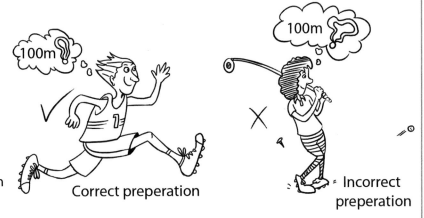

Correct preperation   Incorrect preperation

That is the purpose of this book: to train and fine-tune your skills for success in the National 5 History examination.

How should I use this book?

Well, you've paid your money, so you could use your imagination and do anything you like with the book.

A.   You could prop up the wobbly leg of your table.

•   You could use it as a table tennis bat.

1.   You could use it to hide your stash of Twix bars under.

f)   You could use it to test your ability to do a whole paper in 1 hour 30 minutes to improve your timing.

>   You could use it to work on one particular set of skills needed in one particular part of the paper.

X   You could use one question to test yourself at the end of an hour's revision.

iii.   You could annoy your history teacher by handing in a completed practice paper ALREADY MARKED (with a smiley face saying 'well done' at the end).

Fifthly: You could get inside the mind of the exam marker and use the mark schemes at the end to measure your progress from week to week.

Finally: You could use it to get a top grade in your National 5 examination and never look back on your unstoppable road to success.

What you use this book for of course depends on what you need. You should, from time to time, take stock of the areas that you need to improve on to be successful.

What needs to be improved	How to use this book
I always run out of time	Practice spending no more than about one-and-a-half minutes per mark, then no more than seven minutes on a 5-mark question, then no more than 30 minutes on any one section.
I can't remember the right facts when I need them	Once you have done some revision on a topic, close your books and test yourself on a 'describe' or 'explain' question. Mark it yourself, or get someone to mark it for you using the mark scheme.
I *still* can't remember the right facts when I need them!	Repeat the exercise above every few days – re-revising really works, particularly if it is slightly different each time, e.g. using a different question.
I get muddled when I'm using sources	Try each type of source question first with all of your books and notes open and without worrying about timing. Get used to the different things expected from each question and to the language used in the topics you are doing.
I'm not very confident about the exam	Do these practice papers as a whole or in parts in a place where you feel happy about studying – where you don't feel too much pressure.
I'm *still* not very confident about the exam!	Write down everything you know about one section on a blank sheet of paper. Revise the topic to fill in the gaps. Have a break. Do a paper or a section. Record how you did. A week or so later, come back and do the same thing (you could even do the same questions). See how much you have improved. Feel confident!
My books keep sliding off the side of the table	The table is wobbly. Prop up the leg with a book.

The exam

Your teachers and your class notes will have given you much of the factual information that you need to know about the topics and events in the various sections of the examination. If you feel that you need more information, there is much that you can find online to supplement these sources. You will also note that as a part of the mark schemes in this book there are suggestions for factual information that you might be expected to include. It is important that you are clear about the topics you will be answering on and that you have sufficient knowledge of these topics. There will be a Scottish topic, a British topic and a European and World topic for you to answer.

Don't be tempted to tackle a topic that you have not prepared for, even if you did see an amusing song relating to it on *Horrible Histories* the week before!

Across the three topics you will be asked to address six types of question. Each requires something slightly different from you. The mark schemes point out the marker's expectations of your answer, but here is a brief outline:

1. **Describe something** – you don't need to worry too much about the order of what you write about and you should not use up valuable time explaining its importance or evaluating the role of various factors in your answer. You don't have to be entertaining. Stick to the facts that are relevant and write clearly. If there are five marks available, make five good points about the thing you were asked to describe and move on within seven minutes.

TOP TIP Before you start, quickly write down on a scrap piece of paper five words or phrases that will work as headings for your description. This way you won't miss a point.

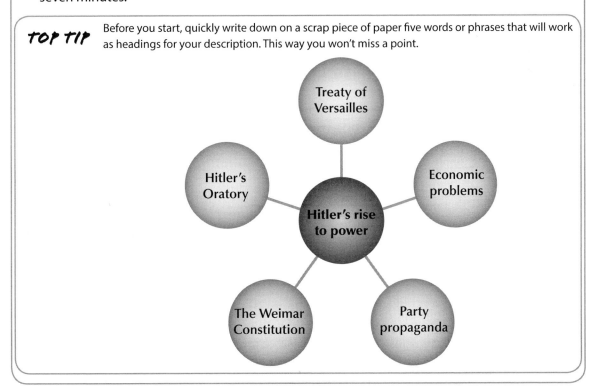

2. **Explain something** – this asks a bit more of you. You must show that you understand why something has occurred and make several different or related points that connect together into an explanation. You can get credit here if you expand one point into a larger point by saying more of significance about it. You don't need to say which part of your explanation was most important however. Again quickly add up your points to see if you have got all of the marks available. If there are 5 marks, you might have made five points, or you may have made three points, two of which you expanded enough to say they were worth 2 marks each. If there are 5 marks available move on after seven minutes.

3. **Evaluate the extent to which a particular factor is important** – this asks a little more of you again. This time you have to identify the various factors in causing something and evaluate the relative importance of the one mentioned in the question. You should spend the most time on the factor mentioned; explain its significance against the others, which also have some importance.

TOP TIP   To help you picture the significance of a particular factor, try doing a 'ripple diagram'. Imagine the factor you are considering is like a stone dropped into a pond. It will have some immediate and obvious effects, then wider ripples, then, possibly longer-term consequences.

STANDARD TIME

GROWTH OF TOWNS

JOINING UP MARKETS

IRON AND COAL INDUSTRIES

CHEAPER TRANSPORT OF RAW MATERIAL

RAILWAYS + INDUSTRIALISATION

FACTORIES INLAND

HOLIDAYS BY SEASIDE / LEASURE INDUSTRIES

NEWSPAPER

ENGINEERING

4. **Evaluate the usefulness of a source in helping you understand an issue or event** – a source-based question asks you to make a judgement about the reliability, value and validity of a source in relation to a specific event or issue. You can get marks for assessing the context or provenance of the source – who wrote it (or drew or photographed it, etc.), when it was created in relation to the events described, the purpose of the source – but also for the language used in the source and by accurately explaining what the source tells you about the issue or event.

TOP TIP

Have a bank of technical words ready for this type of question. Especially when you are trying to say in words whether a pictorial source is useful or not. Having to hand words that you are likely to use when answering this type of question under exam pressure is very helpful. For example:

- Propaganda – 'This poster is a piece of propaganda so it only shows one side of the story.'
- Exaggerated – 'The author of this article has used exaggerated language to make his point.'
- Biased – 'Because the writer here is writing about her deadly enemy she is biased in what she says.'
- Formal – 'This is a formal report of what happened, written in formal language, which makes it more reliable and therefore useful in finding out what happened.'
- Informal – 'Because this was a personal letter, it is not written formally so it is not very precise in what it says.'
- Official – 'This is the official account of what happened, so it is written by someone who was in a position to know what happened.'
- Private – 'This is a private diary, which was not for publication, so the author was being honest in what she said.'
- Public – 'This was for public consumption in a speech and does not reflect what he really thought about this issue.'
- Factual – 'The language used in this account is factual and so can be trusted as a reflection of what the author saw.'
- Opinion – 'This is a newspaper editorial which is simply expressing the opinion of the editor and he does not seem to provide many facts to support it.'
- Satirical – 'This cartoon is satirical, not a literal portrayal of events, and intends to make fun of the man in it. It is useful therefore only to show what some people thought of him.
- Partial – 'Because this person was not in a position to know what would happen the next day, it could only give a partial picture of events so its usefulness is limited.'

5. **Assess how fully a source describes an event or explains an issue** – this asks you to point out both what is mentioned or hinted at in the source and what is not mentioned in the source and then make a judgement about the extent to which the source addresses the issue concerned.

TOP TIP

Think of the source as one piece of a jigsaw. Imagine that you can see the whole picture on the box of the jigsaw (your knowledge of the topic should show you this!). Describe the parts of the jigsaw shown in the piece you can see, then describe the whole picture 'on the box'.

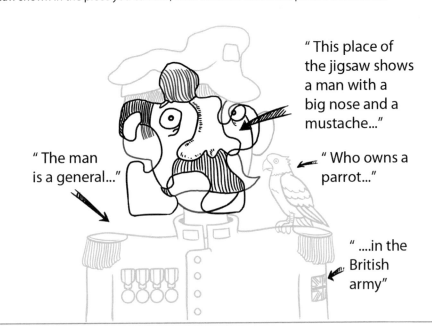

"This place of the jigsaw shows a man with a big nose and a mustache..."

"The man is a general..."

"Who owns a parrot..."

"....in the British army"

6. **Compare how two different sources view a particular event or issue** – this type of question requires you to make direct comparisons between the sources showing both agreement and differences with them. You should be able to find overall differences or similarities as well as smaller individual points.

> ***TOP TIP*** Don't just write about one of the sources and then the other one. Make sure you make your comparisons direct ones.

One last thing: in the Scottish Unit of the National 5 examination you will only be asked questions on three out of the four sub-units of each topic. In these practice papers we have not always followed this rule exactly as for revision and practice it is helpful to review your knowledge of the whole unit.

Good luck! (Something that usually comes from preparation...)

Topic index

Topic	Practice question in:	Knowledge for Prelim			Knowledge for SQA exam		
		Have difficulty	Still need work	Okay	Have difficulty	Still need work	Okay
SECTION 1 – SCOTTISH							
Part A. The Wars of Independence, 1286–1328	Exams A and D (pages 14 and 47)						
Part B. Mary Queen of Scots and the Scottish Reformation, 1542–1587	Exam B (page 24)						
Part C. The Treaty of Union, 1689–1715	Exams C and D (pages 35 and 48)						
Part D. Migration and Empire, 1830–1939	Exam B (page 25)						
Part E. The Era of the Great War, 1910–1928	Exams A and C (pages 15 and 36)						
SECTION 2 – BRITISH							
Part A. The Creation of the Medieval Kingdoms, 1066–1406	Exam A (page 16)						
Part B. War of the Three Kingdoms, 1603–1651	Exams B and D (pages 26 and 49)						
Part C. The Atlantic Slave Trade, 1770–1807	Exam C (pages 37)						
Part D. Changing Britain, 1760–1900	Exams B and D (pages 27 and 50)						
Part E. The Making of Modern Britain, 1880–1951	Exams A and C (pages 17 and 39)						

Topic	Practice question in:	Knowledge for Prelim			Knowledge for SQA exam		
		Have difficulty	Still need work	Okay	Have difficulty	Still need work	Okay
SECTION 3 – EUROPEAN AND WORLD							
Part A. The Cross and the Crescent; the Crusades, 1071–1192	Exam A (page 18)						
Part B. "Tea and Freedom": the American Revolution, 1774–1783	N/A						
Part C. USA 1850–1880	N/A						
Part D. Hitler and Nazi Germany, 1919–1939	Exam A (page 19)						
Part E. Red Flag: Lenin and the Russian Revolution, 1894–1921	Exam B (page 28)						
Part F. Mussolini and Fascist Italy, 1919–1939	Exam D (page 51)						
Part G. Free at Last? Civil Rights in the USA, 1918–1968	Exam C (page 40)						
Part H. Appeasement and the Road to War, 1918–1939	Exam B (page 30)						
Part I. World War II, 1939–1945	Exam C (page 42)						
Part J. The Cold War, 1945–1989	Exam D (page 53)						

Practice Exam A

Practice Papers for SQA Exams

HISTORY

NATIONAL 5

Exam A

Reading for Understanding, Analysis and Evaluation

Duration – 1 hour and 30 minutes

Total marks – 60

SECTION 1 – SCOTTISH – 20 marks

Attempt ONE part.

SECTION 2 – BRITISH – 20 marks

Attempt ONE part.

SECTION 3 – EUROPEAN AND WORLD – 20 marks

Attempt ONE part.

Scotland's leading educational publishers

SECTION 1 – SCOTTISH – 20 marks

Attempt ONE part

Part A – The Wars of Independence, 1286–1328

Attempt the following questions using recalled knowledge and information from the sources where appropriate.

Source A is an extract from The Treaty of Birgham of July 1290, between the Guardians of Scotland and Edward I.

Source A

> We [Edward I] promise… that the kingdom of Scotland shall remain separate and divided from the kingdom of England by its rightful boundaries and borders as has been observed up to now and that it shall be free in itself and independent, reserving always the right of our lord or whoever which has belonged to him or to anyone in the borders elsewhere.

1. Evaluate the usefulness of **Source A** as evidence of how Edward I became involved in Scottish affairs. **5**

   (You may want to comment on who wrote it, when they wrote it, why they wrote it, what they say or what has been missed out.)

2. Describe the role played by John Balliol during the Wars of Independence. **5**

3. Explain the reasons why William Wallace was able to organise resistance to Edward I. **5**

Source B is about the crowning of Robert Bruce as King in 1306.

Source B

> Before committing such a crime in a church, Robert the Bruce had followed a cautious policy to protect his lands and power by supporting Edward I's rule in Scotland.
>
> It is hard to escape the conclusion that the murder of Comyn [led to] Bruce's seizure of the throne as he realised that his best chance of salvation lay in his becoming king, thereby drawing on the natural loyalty which attached to the cause of a legitimate monarch.

4. How fully does **Source B** explain why Bruce fought against Edward I and his son after 1306? (Use **Source B** and recall.) **5**

Part E – The Era of the Great War, 1910–1928

Attempt the following questions using recalled knowledge and information from the sources where appropriate.

Source A describes the use of tanks during the Battle of Cambrai 1917.

Source A

> There were not enough infantry to take advantage of this huge hole in the German defences and the enemy soon began to recover and fight back. By evening many tanks had broken down – over a hundred from lack of petrol or engine failure and another sixty five from enemy gunfire, including sixteen knocked out by a single German field gun. All these tanks were now stranded in German territory and there were no reserves.

1. How fully does **Source A** describe the impact of tanks on war on the Western Front? (Use **Source A** and recall.) **5**

2. Describe the ways in which conscientious objectors were treated during the war. **5**

Source B is from a letter written by Emmeline Pankhurst to a Scottish Suffragette on 10 January 1913.

Source B

> My Dear Friend
>
> The Prime Minister has announced that the Women's Amendments to the Manhood Suffrage Bill will shortly be discussed in Parliament. The WSPU has declined to call any truce on its militant activities on the strength of the Prime Minister's promise to discuss the issue of votes for women. There is no commitment from the government to get the act carried. We must continue to show our determination. Women have been disappointed in the past. We will fight on and cause as much public disorder as we can. The cause is a just cause and it will triumph.

3. Evaluate the usefulness of **Source B** as evidence of the reasons why women won the vote in 1918. **5**

   (You may want to comment on who wrote it, when they wrote it, why they wrote it, what they say or what has been missed out.)

4. Explain the reasons why heavy industry declined in Scotland after the First World War. **5**

SECTION 2 – BRITISH – 20 Marks

Attempt ONE part

Attempt the following questions using recalled knowledge and information from the sources where appropriate.

Part A – The Creation of the Medieval Kingdoms, 1066–1406

Attempt the following questions using recalled knowledge and information from the sources where appropriate.

Source A was written by Gerald of Wales about King Henry II in his book *Concerning the instruction of a Prince*, which he wrote after Henry's death to explain what a good king was. He was a part of his court.

Source A

> He was a man of easy access and patient with those of lesser rank, flexible and witty, second to none in politeness ... Strenuous in warfare ... Very shrewd in civil life ... He was fierce towards those who remained untamed, but merciful towards the defeated, harsh to his servants, expansive towards strangers, spent generously in public, frugal in private... Humble, an oppressor of the nobility and a condemner of the proud.

1. Evaluate the usefulness of **Source A** as evidence of Henry's kingship. **6**

   (You may wish to comment on who wrote it, when they wrote it, why they wrote it, what they say or what has been missed out.)

2. To what extent did monasteries become the most important branch of the medieval church? **8**

3. Explain the reasons why castles were built across Britain under Norman rule. **6**

Part E – The Making of Modern Britain, 1880–1951

Attempt the following questions using recalled knowledge and information from the sources where appropriate.

1. To what extent did Liberal Welfare Reforms 1906–14 successfully address the problem of poverty in Britain in the early 20th century? **8**

2. Explain the reasons why attitudes towards poverty in Britain changed during the Second World War. **6**

Source A is from an editorial in the *Daily Sketch* from February 1948 and refers to Bevan's negotiations with doctors about pay and conditions in the new NHS.

Source A

> The State medical service is part of the Socialist plot to convert Great Britain into a National Socialist economy. The doctors' stand is the first effective revolt of the professional classes against Socialist tyranny. There is nothing that Bevan or any other Socialist can do about it in the shape of Hitlerian coercion.

3. Evaluate the usefulness of **Source A** as evidence of reasons for the introduction of the NHS in 1948. **6**

   (You may want to comment on who wrote it, when they wrote it, why they wrote it, what they say or what has been missed out.)

SECTION 3 – EUROPEAN AND WORLD – 20 marks

Attempt ONE part

Part A – The Cross and the Crescent: the Crusades, 1071–1192

Attempt the following questions using recalled knowledge and information from the sources where appropriate.

Sources A and **B** are about the reasons why people went on the First Crusade.

Source A is an extract from Pope Urban II's sermon at Clermont in 1095.

Source A

This land you inhabit is everywhere shut in by the sea, is surrounded by ranges of mountains and is overcrowded by your numbers ... This is why you devour and fight one another, make war and even kill one another ... Let all dissensions [arguments] be settled. Take the road to the Holy Sepulchre, rescue that land from a dreadful race and rule over it yourselves.

Source B

The preachers foretold confidently that the New Jerusalem would appear on earth when the Old Jerusalem was restored to Christian ownership. They spoke of a golden land, a land of milk and honey, where the rewards to those who helped to regain the Holy City for Christ would be immense.

1. Compare the views of **Sources A** and **B** about why people went on the First Crusade. (Compare the sources overall and/or in detail.)   **4**

2. Describe the course of the People's Crusade.   **5**

3. Explain the reasons for the fall of the Kingdom of Jerusalem to Saladin in 1187.   **5**

Source C describes Richard I towards the end of the Third Crusade.

Source C

During the winter, when Saladin had disbanded most of his forces, Richard took the army on an expedition into the hills. They got to within twelve miles of Jerusalem. But it was clear that even if they took the city, there was no way to hold it once Richard and his army had gone. If they entered Jerusalem and fulfilled their vows, few in his army would be inclined to stay. There were not enough Christian knights who wanted to live out their lives in the Holy Land. With the French King already departed and his brother plotting against him at home, Richard was looking for a way out.

4. How fully does **Source C** explain the problems facing Crusaders on the Third Crusade?   **6**

Part D – Hitler and Nazi Germany, 1919–1939

Attempt the following questions using recalled knowledge and information from the sources where appropriate.

1. Explain the reasons why there was opposition to the Weimar Republic in the early 1920s.   **5**

Sources A and **B** are about the impact of the Great Depression on German politics.

Source A

> Before the crash, 1.25 million people were unemployed in Germany. By the end of 1930 the figure had reached nearly 4 million, 15.3 per cent of the population ... wages also fell and those with full-time work had to survive on lower incomes. Hitler, who was considered a fool in 1928 when he predicted economic disaster, was now seen in a different light.

Source B

> The Depression helped Hitler by undermining [German] democracy. The Republic was governed by coalitions because of the nature of the voting system. The Economic crisis caused the coalition under Muller to fall apart in 1930. The next three Chancellors ... relied on the President's powers ... to rule by decree without the support of the Reichstag. In this undemocratic atmosphere Hitler was able to come to power through the back door.

2. Compare the views of **Sources A** and **B** about the impact of the Great Depression on German politics. (Compare the sources overall and/or in detail.)   **4**

3. Describe the treatment of minority groups in Germany by the Nazis in the 1930s.   **5**

In **Source C** Hitler explains what he expects of young German men.

Source C

> My teaching is hard. Weakness has to be knocked out of them. In my [New Order] a youth will grow up before which the world will shrink back. A violently active dominating, intrepid, brutal youth – that is what I am after. Youth must be all those things. It must be indifferent to pain. There must be no weakness or tenderness in it. I want to see once more in its eyes the gleam of pride and independence of the beast of prey. Strong and handsome must my young men be. I will have them fully trained in all physical exercises. I intend to have an athletic youth – that is the first and the chief thing. In this way I shall eradicate the thousands of years of human domestication. Then I shall have in front of me the pure and noble natural material. With that I can create the new order.

4. How fully does **Source C** explain Nazi policies towards young people in the 1930s? (Use **Source C** and recall.)   **6**

Practice Exam B

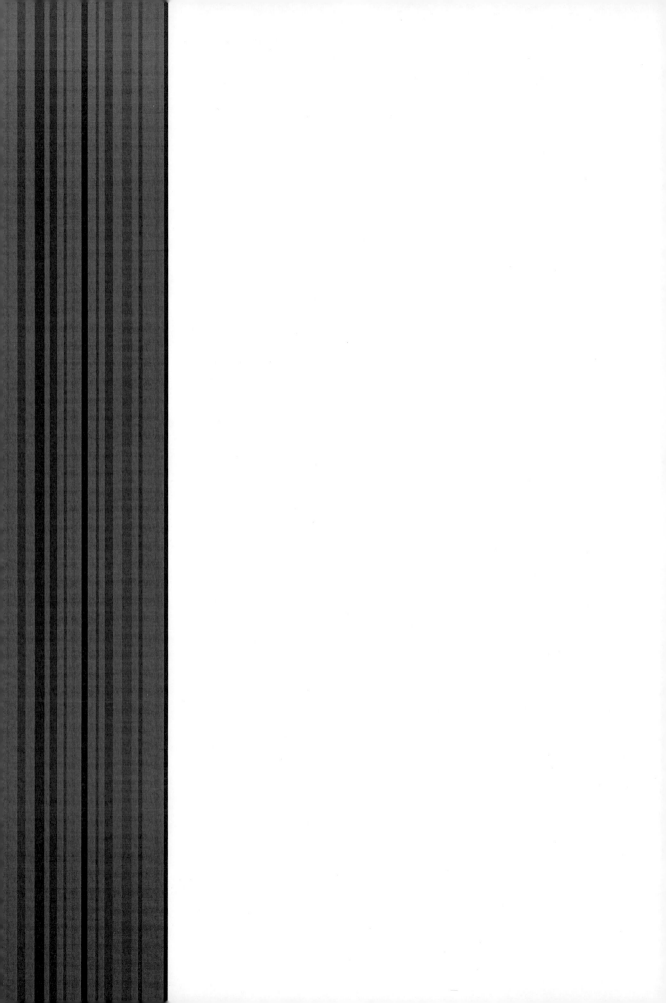

HISTORY

NATIONAL 5

Exam B

Reading for Understanding, Analysis and Evaluation

Duration – 1 hour and 30 minutes

Total marks – 60

SECTION 1 – SCOTTISH – 20 marks

Attempt ONE part.

SECTION 2 – BRITISH – 20 marks

Attempt ONE part.

SECTION 3 – EUROPEAN AND WORLD – 20 marks

Attempt ONE part.

Scotland's leading educational publishers

SECTION 1 – SCOTTISH – 20 marks

Attempt ONE part

Part B – Mary Queen of Scots and the Scottish Reformation, 1542–1587

Attempt the following questions using recalled knowledge and information from the sources where appropriate.

Source A is about the consequences of the Rough Wooing.

Source A

The costs of the war are hard to assess. Government and society stood up well to seven years of garrisoning, forced quarter and violence. The Church suffered the most, but the effects were mixed: the occupation had greatly accelerated the spread of Protestant literature, which would later be blamed ... as the principal cause of the spread of heresy (reformation ideas), but collaboration with the English had also helped to drive the movement underground.

1. How fully does **Source A** explain the impact of the "Rough Wooing" on Scotland?   **5**

2. Describe the role of John Knox in the reformation in Scotland.   **5**

In **Source B** Mary Queen of Scots tried to communicate a message to Queen Elizabeth explaining her actions after the murder of Darnley.

Source B

I am more upset than anyone at the tragic death of my husband: if my subjects had allowed me to act and if they had given me free use of my authority as Queen, I would have punished those responsible. I had no knowledge of who those people were and none of my subjects told me that those who are now held to be guilty of carrying out this crime were the ones most responsible for committing it; if they had done, I would certainly not have acted as I have up to now. I believe that I have done nothing except at the advice of the nobility of the realm.

3. Evaluate the usefulness of **Source B** as evidence of Mary Queen of Scots' actions at the time of the murder of Darnley.   **5**

    (You may want to comment on who wrote it, when they wrote it, why they wrote it, what they say or what has been missed out.)

4. Explain the reasons why Mary Queen of Scots was executed in 1587.   **5**

Part D – Migration and Empire, 1830–1939

Attempt the following questions using recalled knowledge and information from the sources where appropriate.

1. Explain the reasons why people from Ireland and Europe arrived in Scotland in the 19th century.   **5**

Source A is about migration from the Highlands and Lowlands of Scotland in the 19th Century.

Source A

> There was undoubtedly coercion (use of force), with the many in arrears over their rent being offered a choice of a free passage or eviction from their crofts. Between 1841 and 1861 the population of the West Coast above Ardnamurchan and the Inner and Outer Hebrides went down by a third. After that, though emigration continued apace, it was largely from the Lowlands, driven not by destitution (extreme poverty), but by the prospect of better opportunities.

2. How fully does **Source A** explain the reasons for migration from Scotland in the 19th century?   **5**

Source B is an account of Irish sugar-workers in Greenock, 1836, from a Report on the State of the Irish Poor in Great Britain, Parliamentary Papers.

Source B

> Mr Thomas Fairrie, sugar manufacturer, of Greenock [stated] 'If it was not for the Irish, we should be obliged to import Germans, as is done in London. The Scotch will not work in sugar-houses; the heat drives them away in the first fortnight. If it was not for the Irish, we should be forced to give up trade; and the same applies to every sugar-house in town. This is a well-known fact. Germans would be our only resource, and we could not readily get them. Highlanders would not do the work'.

3. Evaluate the usefulness of **Source B** as evidence of the reaction to Irish immigrants in Scotland.   **5**

    (You may want to comment on who wrote it, when they wrote it, why they wrote it, what they say or what has been missed out.)

4. Describe the role played by Scots in the development of the British Empire between 1830 and 1939.   **5**

SECTION 2 – BRITISH – 20 Marks

Attempt ONE part

Part C – War of the Three Kingdoms, 1603–1651

Attempt the following questions using recalled knowledge and information from the sources where appropriate.

Source A is from a speech given by King James VI/I to Parliament, March 1610.

Source A

> The state of monarchy is the supreme thing upon earth; for kings are not only God's lieutenants on earth and sit upon God's throne, but even by God himself are called gods. There are three things that illustrate the nature of monarchy: one from the Bible, the others from policy and philosophy. In the Scriptures kings are called gods and so their power can be compared to the divine power. Kings are also compared to the fathers of families, for the king truly is father of his country, the political father of his people. And lastly, kings are compared to the head of this microcosm (small model) of the body of man.

1. Evaluate the usefulness of **Source B** as evidence of the nature of Royal Authority 1603–25. **6**

   (You may want to comment on who wrote it, when they wrote it, why they wrote it, what they say or what has been missed out.)

2. To what extent did challenges to Royal Authority in Scotland cause the outbreak of war between Charles I and English Parliamentarians in 1641? **8**

3. Explain the reasons why King Charles I was executed in 1649. **6**

Part D – Changing Britain, 1760–1900

Attempt the following questions using recalled knowledge and information from the sources where appropriate.

1. Explain the reasons for housing problems in British cities in the first half of the 19th century. **6**

Source A is from an article in the *Scottish Railway Gazette* for April 1845.

Source A

> Railways will mean that all parts of the country will become more opened up. Land in the interior will, by a system of cheap and rapid transport for manure and farm produce, become almost as valuable as land on the coast. The man of business can as easily join his family at a distance of 10 or 12 miles as could formerly be done at 2 or 3 miles.

2. Evaluate the usefulness of **Source A** as evidence of the impact of railways on Britain. **6**

   (You may want to comment on who wrote it, when they wrote it, why they wrote it, what they say or what has been missed out.)

3. To what extent was Parliamentary Reform in the 19th century brought about by the actions of radical protesters? **8**

SECTION 3 – European and World – 20 Marks

Attempt ONE part

Part E – Red Flag: Lenin and the Russian Revolution, 1894–1921

Attempt the following questions using recalled knowledge and information from the sources where appropriate.

1. Describe the problems facing Russian agriculture and industry before 1905.

   5

Sources A and **B** describe the Tsar's government of Russia between 1905 and 1914.

Source A

> The Tsar felt forced to promise a kind of constitution in October 1905. The Duma was very weak: it could not make laws, the Council of Ministers was selected by the Tsar and elections to the Duma were rigged to ensure that the nobility had the strongest representation and the more radical liberals were excluded. Even so, the Tsar resented sharing his ancient autocratic powers with anybody else. Having stepped away from the old ways of ruling, he tried to avoid having to deal with the Duma, cutting back its powers even more when he had the chance.

Source B

> The half-hearted concessions that the Tsar made in 1905 to share power with society represented by political parties neither made the regime more popular with the opposition nor raised his prestige with the people at large. They could not understand how a proper ruler could allow himself to be openly criticised by another government institution. His divine right to rule depended on his ability to rule forcefully. Nicholas II fell not because he was hated, but because he was held in contempt.

2. Compare the views of **Sources A** and **B** about the Tsar's government of Russia between 1905 and 1914. (Compare the sources overall and/or in detail.)

   4

Source C is about Order No. 1 issued on 1 March 1917.

Source C

> The Petrograd Soviet effectively controlled transport and communications and workers and soldiers looked to it for leadership. There was therefore 'dual power' because, while the Soviet was happy for the Provisional Government of the Duma to take control of the government, the Soviet itself had many of the reins of power. On 1 March it issued Army Order No 1: no one should do what the Provisional Government said unless the Soviet agreed.

3. How fully does **Source C** explain the failure of the Provisional Government in 1917? (Use **Source C** and recall.)   **6**

4. Explain the reasons why the Bolsheviks defeated the White forces in the Civil War.   **5**

MARKS

Part H – Appeasement and the Road to War, 1918–1939

Attempt the following questions using recalled knowledge and information from the sources where appropriate.

Source A is about the Treaty of Versailles, signed in June 1918.

Source A

Germany was given two choices: either to sign the Treaty or to be invaded by the Allies.

They signed the Treaty as in reality they had no choice. When the ceremony was over, Clemenceau went out into the gardens of Versailles and said, "it is a beautiful day".

The Treaty seemed to satisfy the "Big Three" as in their eyes it was a just peace as it kept Germany weak yet strong enough to stop the spread of communism; kept the French border with Germany safe from another German attack and created the organisation, the League of Nations, that would end warfare throughout the world.

However, it left a mood of anger throughout Germany as it was felt that as a nation Germany had been unfairly treated.

1. How fully does **Source A** explain the consequences of the Treaty of Versailles? (Use **Source A** and recall.) **6**

2. Explain the reasons why the Nazis adopted an aggressive foreign policy in the 1930s. **5**

Sources B and **C** are about the reasons why Britain adopted a policy of Appeasement towards Germany in the 1930s.

Source B

The Government was concerned with the weakness of its armed forces, notably the lack of home defences, especially against the bomber. There had been widespread disarmament in the 1920s; there were no troops immediately available to mount a challenge.

The heads of Britain's armed forces – Chiefs of Staff – consistently warned Chamberlain that Britain was too weak to fight. Alongside this Nazi propaganda encouraged Britain and France to believe that Germany's forces were a lot stronger than they really were.

Source C

> Appeasement was a reasonable response to the problems facing Britain in the 1930s. The British Empire stretched around almost a quarter of the globe and despite the strains of defending such an extensive area, dominion governments expressed limited enthusiasm for helping the mother country if drawn into a major conflict in Europe. The cost of defending an overseas empire with a strong navy conflicted with the demands of defending Britain from aerial threats and the possibility of a land war in Europe. Meanwhile there remained a strong pacifist mood in British society that politicians could not ignore.

3. Compare the views of **Sources B** and **C** about the reasons for the British policy of Appeasement. (Compare the sources overall and/or in detail.)   **4**

4. Describe the attempts to address German demands over Czechoslovakia in 1938.   **5**

Practice Exam C

HISTORY

NATIONAL 5

Exam C

Reading for Understanding, Analysis and Evaluation

Duration – 1 hour and 30 minutes

Total marks – 60

SECTION 1 – SCOTTISH – 20 marks

Attempt ONE part.

SECTION 2 – BRITISH – 20 marks

Attempt ONE part.

SECTION 3 – EUROPEAN AND WORLD – 20 marks

Attempt ONE part.

Scotland's leading educational publishers

SECTION 1 – SCOTTISH – 20 marks

Attempt ONE part

Part C – The Treaty of Union, 1689–1715

Attempt the following questions using recalled knowledge and information from the sources where appropriate.

Source A is about the Worcester Affair, which was a part of the increasing tensions between Scotland and England in the years before the Act of Union.

Source A

> The seizure of the Annandale increased ill feeling in Scotland. In July 1704 an English ship, the Worcester, anchored at Leith. The directors of the Company of Scotland, thinking she was an East India Company ship, seized her in exchange for the Annandale. Suspicions were aroused that she had played a part in the loss of another Company ship, the Speedy Return, off the coast of Africa in1703. In September 1704, Captain Green and the crew of the Worcester were arrested and charged with piracy and murder. The Admiralty Court jury consisted of Edinburgh merchants and sea captains, some of whom were shareholders in the Company of Scotland. In March 1705, despite a lack of evidence against them, Green and two of his men were sentenced to death.

1. How fully does **Source A** explain the reasons for tension between England and Scotland before 1707? (Use **Source A** and recall.) **5**

Source B is by John Erskine, Earl of Mar, Secretary of State in Scotland, writing a letter to the Earl of Godolphin, Lord Treasurer of England, 16 September, 1706.

Source B

> When I came here first, there were very few people in town, so I went to my country house and stayed till last Saturday. I talked with a great many and found most of them against the Union, but when I told them what it was and the advantages they did not expect such terms, so that most of them were mightily softened and some entirely converted.

2. Evaluate the usefulness of **Source B** as evidence of how Scots felt about the Act of Union. **5**

   (You may want to comment on who wrote it, when they wrote it, why they wrote it, what they say or what has been missed out.)

3. Describe the role of the Duke of Hamilton in the passage of the Treaty of Union. **5**

4. Explain the reasons for the Jacobite rebellion of 1715. **5**

Part E – The Era of the Great War, 1910–1928

Attempt the following questions using recalled knowledge and information from the sources where appropriate.

Source A is about recruitment to the British Army during World War One.

Source A

Usually the rush of Scots to join the army in 1914 is put down to enthusiasm and patriotic fervour. Following the call from Parliament for 100 000 men to join the British Expeditionary Force, the army was overwhelmed with 750 000 volunteers in the first six weeks. By January over a million had joined up. While defence of 'King and Country' was important to many, others were pushed to join up by the wish to escape unemployment or through the encouragement of employers or others, not to mention the peer pressure created by the formation of "Pals' Battalions" in towns, villages and workplaces.

1. How fully does **Source A** explain the motives of those volunteering for the army in the first year of World War One? (Use **Source A** and recall.) **5**

2. Explain the reasons why Scottish industries were important to the war effort in World War One. **5**

3. Describe the impact of the Defence of the Realm Act on people living in Scotland. **5**

Source B is from the pamphlet "Manifesto of the Joint Strike Committee, Glasgow: a call to British Labour", 31 January 1919.

Source B

Dastardly attempt to smash Trade Unionism

The Joint Committee. ... initiated the movement for a Forty Hours week with a view to absorbing the unemployed. A strike for this object began on 27th January. This has the support of Trades Unionists all over the British Isles. ... (On Friday 31st January) The bludgeon attack on the strikers … was deliberately ordered by the officers and was unprovoked. The attack was sheer brutality by the police to satisfy the lust of the masters for broken skulls.

4. Evaluate the usefulness of **Source B** as evidence of disturbances on Clydeside. **5**

   (You may want to comment on who wrote it, when they wrote it, why they wrote it, what they say or what has been missed out.)

SECTION 2 – BRITISH – 20 Marks

Attempt ONE part

Part C – The Atlantic Slave Trade, 1770–1807

Attempt the following questions using recalled knowledge and information from the sources where appropriate.

1. Explain the impact of the Triangular Trade on the British economy. **6**

Source A is a court record from Dominica, part of the British Colony in the Leeward Islands, January 1814.

Source A

1814 Jan[uar]y 15	John Pierre	Mr Grano	Co[ur]t Martial	Attempting to return to the Runaways with Provisions & having been runaway 2 Months	To be hanged	Hanged: Head cut off & put on a Pole. Body hanged on a Gibbet, 16 Jan[uar]y 1814
	Sarah	ditto	ditto	ditto	To receive 50 lashes	Pardoned & released 30th Jan[uar]y
	Hetty, Penny & Placide	ditto	ditto	ditto	To receive 40 lashes each	Received 40 lashes each & returned to owner's att[ention] 22nd Jan[uar]y
28	Joseph	Mr Dubocq	ditto	supplying Runaways with salt & with provisions	Not guilty	Discharged
	Pierre	Mr Polus Estate	ditto	Encouraging the Neg[roe]s upon that estate who had absconded to stay away	To receive 100 lashes & to be worked in chains 6 months	Rec[eived] 100 lashes & died in Jail 6 april
	Charles	Mr Bonnjean	ditto	Being runaway near 17 months	ditto	Rec[eived] 100 lashes

2. Evaluate the usefulness of **Source A** in explaining the treatment of slaves on Caribbean plantations.

   (You may want to comment on who wrote it, when they wrote it, why they wrote it, what they say or what has been missed out.)

   6

3. To what extent can the abolition of the slave trade be explained by the actions of abolitionist campaigners in Parliament?

   8

Part E – The Making of Modern Britain, 1880–1951

Attempt the following questions using recalled knowledge and information from the sources where appropriate.

Source A is from Seebohm Rowntree's survey of poverty in York, published in 1901.

Source A

We have been accustomed to look upon the poverty in London as exceptional. However, the result of careful investigation shows the proportion of poverty in London is practically equalled in what is a typical provincial town. We are faced with the startling probability that from 25 to 30% of the urban population in the United Kingdom are living in poverty.

That in this land of incredible wealth, in a time of such prosperity never seen before, over a quarter of the population lives in poverty is a fact that may well cause great heart searching.

1. Evaluate the usefulness of **Source A** in explaining changing attitudes towards poverty in Britain.   **6**

   (You may want to comment on who wrote it, when they wrote it, why they wrote it, what they say or what has been missed out.)

2. Explain why the Liberal government introduced reforms to improve the lives of children and the old.   **6**

3. To what extent could the creation of the National Health Service be said to be the most successful of the Labour Government's measures between 1945–51?   **8**

SECTION 3 – European and World – 20 marks

Attempt ONE part

Part G – Free at last? Civil Rights in the USA, 1918–1968

Attempt the following questions using recalled knowledge and information from the sources where appropriate.

Sources A and **B** are about immigration into America.

Source A

American magazine, *The Atlantic Monthly*, 1907

This horde of immigrants has mainly come since the Irish potato famine of the middle of the last century. The rapid increase year by year has taken the form, not of a steady growth, but of an intermittent flow. First came the people of the British Isles ... These were succeeded by the Germans...

More recent still are the Italians, beginning with a modest 20,000 in 1876, rising to over 200,000 arrivals in 1888, and constituting an army of 300,000 in the single year of 1907: and accompanying the Italian has come the great horde of Slavs, Huns, and Jews.

It is the last great wave which has most alarmed us in America.

Source B

After 1890 Italians, Poles, Jews, and Slavs – ethnic groups rarely encountered en masse earlier in American history – arrived in large numbers. Although very many went home again and over 85% of the population remained native born, a significant number settled in America.

Immigrants in New York, Chicago and San Francisco tended to congregate together with their countrymen ... However, during the 1920s – the chain store, the bank branch, the national radio broadcast, and the Hollywood motion picture created, in some cases for the first time, a real common ground that crossed ethnic boundaries in America's cities.

1. Compare the views of **Sources A** and **B** about the nature of immigration into America. (Compare the sources overall and/or in detail.) **4**

2. Describe the activities and influence of the Ku Klux Klan in America after 1918. **5**

3. Explain the reasons for the passage of the Civil Rights Act 1964. **5**

Source C is about the Black Panther Party.

Source C

The Panthers were strongly influenced by Stokley Carmichael, Chairman of the SNCC who had called on "...black people in this country to unite, to recognize their heritage, to build a sense of community. It is a call for black people to define their own goals, to lead their own organizations." .... The Black Panthers focused more upon grass roots action, such as their Free Breakfast for Children program and their campaigns against police brutality. Their military-style uniforms and militant language seemed intimidating to many mainstream Americans and J Edgar Hoover, Director of the FBI called them "the greatest threat to the internal security of the country".

4. How fully does **Source C** explain the impact of militant campaigns for civil rights in America? (Use **Source C** and recall.)　　　　　　　　　　　　　　　　**6**

Part I – World War II, 1939–1945

Attempt the following questions using recalled knowledge and information from the sources where appropriate.

1. Explain the reasons for the success of the tactic of Blitzkreig in the early months of World War Two.

5

Sources A and **B** are about the Japanese attack on Pearl Harbour in November 1941.

Source A

While occupying French Indochina in July 1941, Japan knew that a full-scale invasion of South-east Asia would prompt war with America. It needed a mechanism to buy itself sufficient time and space to conquer successfully crucial targets like the Philippines, Burma and Malaya. The attack on Pearl Harbor was that mechanism; merely a means to an end. By destroying its Pacific Fleet, Japan expected to remove America from the Pacific equation for long enough to allow it to secure the resources it needed so desperately and hoped to crush American morale sufficiently to prompt Roosevelt to sue for peace.

Source B

The Japanese were tired of negotiations with the United States. They wanted to continue their expansion within Asia but the United States had placed an extremely restrictive embargo on Japan in the hopes of curbing Japan's aggression. Negotiations to solve their differences hadn't been going well.

Rather than giving in to U.S. demands, the Japanese decided to launch a surprise attack against the United States in an attempt to destroy the United States' naval power even before an official announcement of war was given.

2. Compare the views of **Sources A** and **B** about the reasons for the Japanese attack on Pearl Harbour (Compare the sources overall and/or in detail).

4

Source C is about Nazi-occupied Europe.

Source C

The harshness of Nazi occupation varied according to the status of the occupied land. In *Mein Kampf*, Hitler had made plain his racial theories: he hated the Jews and Slavs and believed in the 'supremacy' of the Aryan race. It was therefore those unfortunate enough to live to the East of Germany who experienced the greatest cruelty. In the west the Germans were content to take control, using local politicians if possible. In Norway for example, Major Quisling took charge; and in the area of France not occupied by the Germans (Vichy France) the French First World War hero, Marshal Petain, headed the government. Even in the west, however, Nazi rule was backed up by terror tactics enforced by the hated Gestapo and black-uniformed SS.

3. How fully does **Source C** explain the experience of those living under German occupation in World War Two? (Use **Source C** and recall.) **6**

4. Describe the role of the Russian Army in bringing about the defeat of Germany. **5**

Practice Exam D

Practice Papers for SQA Exams

HISTORY

NATIONAL 5

Exam D

Reading for Understanding, Analysis and Evaluation

Duration – 1 hour and 30 minutes

Total marks – 60

SECTION 1 – SCOTTISH – 20 marks

Attempt ONE part.

SECTION 2 – BRITISH – 20 marks

Attempt ONE part.

SECTION 3 – EUROPEAN AND WORLD – 20 marks

Attempt ONE part.

Scotland's leading educational publishers

SECTION 1 – SCOTTISH – 20 marks

Attempt ONE part

Part A – The Wars of Independence, 1286–1328

Attempt the following questions using recalled knowledge and information from the sources where appropriate.

1. Describe the problems caused for Scotland by the death of Alexander III. **5**

2. Explain the reasons for the Franco-Scottish treaty of October 1295. **5**

Source A is about the Scottish uprising against Edward in 1297.

Source A

> Although the origins of the revolt of 1297 have been known to historians for a long time, the idea persists that it was a spontaneous rebellion of landless peasants led by Wallace. It is true that many of the Scottish nobility were in English prisons or had been killed in previous battles. The first outbreaks happened in the north rather than in Wallace's territory. Together Murray, son of a baron and leader of the northern rising, and Wallace were acknowledged as 'commanders of the army of the community of the realm'. Neither a general nor a guerrilla by instinct, Wallace nonetheless deserves to be remembered as an unflinching patriot and a charismatic warlord. That was why the community entrusted him with sole Guardianship of the realm in the Spring of 1298.

3. How fully does **Source A** explain the role played by William Wallace in the Wars of Independence? (Use **Source A** and recall.) **5**

Source B is from the *Lanercrost Chronicle*, a history of the Wars of Independence written shortly afterwards by monks living in a priory in the north of England. It describes the Battle of Bannockburn.

Source B

> When both armies engaged each other and the great horses of the English charged the pikes of the Scots like into a dense forest, there arose a great and terrible crash of spears broken and of the horses wounded to death. Now the English in the rear could not reach the Scots because the leading division was in the way, nor could they do anything to help themselves, so there was nothing for it but to take flight. This account I heard from a trustworthy person who was present as an eyewitness.

4. Evaluate the usefulness of **Source B** in explaining the reasons for Bruce's victory at Bannockburn. **5**

   (You may want to comment on who wrote it, when they wrote it, why they wrote it, what they say or what has been missed out.)

Part C – The Treaty of Union, 1689–1715

Attempt the following questions using recalled knowledge and information from the sources where appropriate.

1. Describe the problems caused for Scotland by the failure of the Darien Scheme.   **5**

Source A discusses the reasons for the introduction of the Treaty of Union.

Source A

> Those who hold the idea that Union was bound to happen have to take into account the particular circumstances that brought it about. It needed a freak coincidence of short-term factors that actually made the passage of a union bill possible. In 1702 there was virtually no support in the English parliament for a union; by 1704 circumstances pointed to a treaty to secure the succession being the most likely outcome. In the autumn of 1708 the position of the Whigs, architects of the Union's passage through Parliament were in trouble and losing support because of the cost of the War of the Spanish Succession and they would not have risked anything as risky as the Act of Union. The bill passed in the eye of a storm that made the unlikely a certainty.

2. How fully does **Source A** explain the reasons for the successful passage of the Treaty of Union?   **5**

3. Explain the reasons for unrest in Edinburgh and elsewhere during the passage of the Treaty of Union.   **5**

Source B is from a letter written by the Earl of Mar to the Earl of Oxford in 1711 discussing his feelings following the Treaty of Union.

Source B

> I am not yet weary of the Union, but still think that if used well [it is] for the good of the whole island and also that it is the only thing which can preserve Scotland, and England too, from Blood and confusion, so I do not at all repent the part I had in it. But should that hardship of the Peeradge (taxation) be put upon us against all sense, reason and fair dealing and if our trade is not more encouraged than it has been so far, or seems likely at the moment, how is it possible that flesh and blood can bear it and what Scots man will not be weary of the union and do all he can to get rid of it?

4. Evaluate the usefulness of **Source B** in explaining the impact of the Treaty of Union in Scotland.   **5**

   (You may want to comment on who wrote it, when they wrote it, why they wrote it, what they say or what has been missed out.)

SECTION 2 – British – 20 marks

Attempt ONE part

Part B – War of the Three Kingdoms, 1603–1651

Attempt the following questions using recalled knowledge and information from the sources where appropriate.

1. Explain the reasons for conflict between the Crown and Parliament in the reign of James I.   **6**

2. To what extent did Charles I's own actions create the crisis that led to war in 1642?   **8**

Source A is from a book of essays by John Selden, who fought in the Civil War, written in 1689.

Source A

> If men would say they took arms for anything but religion, they might have been put off by reasoning; but when they fight for that reason they never can be.
>
> At the heart of pretending that religion is the cause of all wars is because it is the one thing to be found that all men might have an interest in. In this the poor groom might have as much interest as the lord. If they were to fight for land one owns a thousand acres and the other just one; the latter would not risk as much as the one who has a thousand. But religion means as much to both. Had all men the same amount of land by some agrarian law, then all men would say they fought for land.

3. Evaluate the usefulness of **Source A** as evidence of the reasons soldiers used to choose sides in the civil war.   **6**

    (You may want to comment on who wrote it, when they wrote it, why they wrote it, what they say or what has been missed out.)

Part D – Changing Britain, 1760–1900

Attempt the following questions using recalled knowledge and information from the sources where appropriate.

Source A is from a Factory Inspector's report, written in 1836.

Source A

They stated to me that they commenced work on Friday morning and ... they did not cease working until four o'clock on Saturday evening, having been two days and a night thus engaged. I asked every boy the same questions and from each received the same answers. I then went into the house to look at the time book and, in the presence of the masters, referred to the cruelty of the case and stated that I should certainly punish it with all the severity in my power. Mr Rayner, the certificated surgeon of Bastile was with me at the time.

1. Evaluate the usefulness of **Source A** as evidence of the impact of technology and legislation on textile factories in Britain.   **6**

   (You may want to comment on who wrote it, when they wrote it, why they wrote it, what they say or what has been missed out.)

2. Explain the reasons for radical unrest in the first half of the 19th century in Britain.   **6**

3. To what extent were changes to industry in Britain the result of developments in transport?   **8**

SECTION 3 – EUROPEAN AND WORLD – 20 Marks

Attempt ONE part

Part F: Mussolini and Fascist Italy, 1919–1939

Attempt the following questions using recalled knowledge and information from the sources where appropriate.

1. Explain the reasons for the weakness of the Italian state in 1919. **5**

Sources A and **B** are about Mussolini's domestic policies.

Source A

> When Mussolini became Prime Minister in October 1922, he had to tackle the problems that had confronted the Italian state throughout its existence. In terms of domestic policy, it might be argued that Mussolini was more successful than his predecessors in one respect. By direct and ruthless political methods, he put an end to the divisions and in-fighting that had marked Italian politics throughout the previous century. His great talent, perhaps his only talent, was the acquisition and advertisement of power.

Source B

> Mussolini's declared policy was not of course simply to extend his own power. Against communist encouragement of class warfare as a means to a new society, he preached the need to unite all classes in service to the existing state. An upholder of private property and differences in wealth and status, he nevertheless believed that the welfare of the individual should be strictly subordinate to that of the nation. These ideas underlay the gradual development of what the Fascists called 'the corporate state' ... Greater political stability, the fast increasing industrial prosperity and the beginning of a great new programme of public works helped to commend Mussolini whole-heartedly to the Italian people.

2. Compare the views of **Sources A** and **B** about Mussolini's domestic social and economic policies. (Compare the sources overall and/or in detail). **4**

Source C is about the Abyssinian crisis of 1935–6.

Source C

Encouraged no doubt by the ease with which Japan had got her way over Manchuria, Italy, which had long coveted the only large tract of Africa still ruled by Africans, in October 1935 invaded Abyssinia. Preparations had been going on for many months, and doubtless Mussolini thought that his friends the British and French were prepared to turn a blind eye. This time, however, the powers, partly impelled by public opinion, resolved to do something more than protest. The League invoked Article XVI and economic sanctions were quickly applied against Italy. But the policy was not wholeheartedly pressed ... The French premier, Pierre Laval, and the British Foreign Secretary, Sir Samuel Hoare, concocted a compromise scheme by which Italy would be allowed one large part of Abyssinia as an outright possession and another large part as a zone of economic expansion and development.

3. How fully does **Source C** explain the impact of the Abyssinian crisis on Italian foreign policy? (Use **Source C** and recall.) **6**

4. Describe the means by which the Fascist government suppressed opposition to the government. **5**

Part J – The Cold War, 1945–1989

Attempt the following questions using recalled knowledge and information from the sources where appropriate.

Source A is about relations between America and the Soviet Union at the end of World War II.

Source A

> Despite contrasting ideologies, in 1945 the Cold War in Europe had not yet taken its final form. Although under Roosevelt and Truman there was growing suspicion, their inclination was to work with the Soviets and they were under pressure to disengage from European affairs. Stalin was not bent on unlimited expansion, however, and was content to allow British control over Greece. The Cold War took shape most of all over the treatment of Germany. While The USSR stripped resources from Eastern Germany, Stalin saw the American Marshall Plan as a fundamental threat to his strategy for securing the defence of the Soviet Union.

1. How fully does **Source A** explain the reasons for the development of the Cold War in Europe after 1945? (Use **Source A** and recall.) **6**

Sources B and **C** are about the building of the Berlin Wall in 1961.

Source B

> East Germany remained an artificial state and the appeal of its neighbour was enhanced by the accessibility of West German TV in most of the GDR. Denied true democracy, East Germans voted with their feet. In the 1950s the GDR was the only Soviet Bloc country to decline in population, from 19 million to 17 million, as people slipped through the unchecked exits into West Berlin and thence to the Federal Republic.
>
> Faced with this haemorrhage of personnel, Ulbricht finally persuaded Moscow to seal off the city and begin the Berlin Wall on 13 August 1961.

Source C

> In 1961 a new Soviet leader, Nikita Khrushchev, again felt confident enough to try to challenge the West over Berlin. He felt that the new US president, John Kennedy, was weak, as Khrushchev had scored a propaganda victory over the USA the previous year by shooting down an American U2 spy plane and publicly displaying its pilot, Gary Powers. By August 1961, 3000 refugees per day were pouring from impoverished East Berlin into West Berlin. Khrushchev tried to bully Kennedy into withdrawing from West Berlin. When this failed he ordered the building of a wall to cut West Berlin in two.

2. Compare the views of **Sources B** and **C** about the reasons for the building of the Berlin Wall. (Compare the sources overall and/or in detail).   **4**

3. Explain the failure of American forces to defeat the Vietcong in the Vietnam War.   **5**

4. Describe the development of the policy of Detente between the Superpowers in the 1970s and 1980s.   **5**

SECTION 1 – SCOTTISH

Part A – The Wars of Independence, 1286–1328

Source A is an extract from The Treaty of Birgham July 1290, between the Guardians of Scotland and Edward I.

Source A

> We [Edward I] promise… that the kingdom of Scotland shall remain separate and divided from the kingdom of England by its rightful boundaries and borders as has been observed up to now and that it shall be free in itself and independent, reserving always the right of our lord or whoever which has belonged to him or to anyone in the borders elsewhere.

1. Evaluate the usefulness of **Source A** as evidence of how Edward I became involved in Scottish affairs.   **5**

    (You may want to comment on who wrote it, when they wrote it, why they wrote it, what they say or what has been missed out.)

Candidates must evaluate the extent to which a source is useful by commenting on evidence such as the author, type of source, purpose and timing, content and omission.

For a mark to be given, the candidate must identify an aspect of the source and make a comment which shows how this aspect of the source makes the source more or less useful.

Up to the total mark allocation for this question: a maximum of 4 marks can be given for evaluative comments relating to author, type of source, purpose and timing. A maximum of 2 marks may be given for evaluative comments relating to the content of the source. A maximum of 2 marks may be given for points of significant omission.

Candidates can be credited in a number of ways up to a maximum of 5 marks.

Candidates must make a judgement about the usefulness of the source and support this by making evaluative comments on identified aspects of the source.

One mark will be given for each relevant comment made, up to a maximum of 5 marks in total.

Examples of aspects of the source and relevant comments

Author: The Guardians in agreement with Edward I.
Comment:

*   In one sense it is not useful because Edward I would later go back on what he promised in the Treaty of Birgham.

*   However, it states first-hand Edward's public intentions towards Scotland.

Type of source: A legal treaty between the Guardians and Edward.
Comment: This is useful because it is the document that gives Edward a legal interest in Scotland's future, with the consent of Scotland's leaders.

Purpose: To agree the future marriage of the Maid of Norway and Edward's son.
Comment:

- This is useful because it shows Edward wants to bring the English and Scottish kingdoms closer.

- But at this point most of the leading Scots still agree with bringing England and Scotland closer through marriage.

Timing: 1290
Comment:

- The Maid of Norway was very young and Scotland was in a difficult position.

- It is useful because it helps to explain why the Guardians were so keen to get Edward involved.

- It was not yet clear what kind of person Edward was.

- This seemed a good way to provide security and stability for Scotland.

Content: Guarantees the independence of the Scottish kingdom even if the crowns are united in a future marriage.
Comment:

- This is useful in that it suggests some suspicion of the Guardians about Edward's future intentions.

- It is less useful because it does not reveal Edward's actual ambitions.

Points of significant omission:

- Edward believes that even if Scotland is separate and independent, the Scots king is a vassal of the King of England.

- The unexpected death of Margaret on Orkney shortly afterwards meant that the Treaty would come to nothing.

- Edward was invited by the Guardians to settle the 'Great Cause'.

2. Describe the role played by John Balliol during the Wars of Independence.   **5**

Candidates must make a number of relevant, factual points. These should be key points. The points do not need to be in any particular order. The candidate may provide a number of straightforward points or a smaller number of developed points, or a combination of these.

Up to the total mark allocation for this question: 1 mark should be given for each accurate relevant point of knowledge. A second mark should be given for any point that is developed.

Candidates can be credited in a number of ways up to a maximum of 5 marks. They may take different perspectives on the events and may describe a variety of different aspects of the events.

Possible points of knowledge may include:

- John Balliol was chosen, probably correctly, as King by Edward in the Great Cause.

- Later he would be known by some as 'Toom Tabard' because of Edward's stripping of his emblems of kingship in 1296 at Montrose.

- He did homage to Edward as overlord at Newcastle in December 1292.

- John stood up to Edward over the authority of Edward to overrule judgements in the Scottish King's courts.

- Demand for help in Edward's war with France refused by lords at Stirling – Council of the Twelve making decisions rather than Balliol.

- 'Auld' alliance with France, October 1295, and invasion of England led to war.

- Balliol's/ Scottish forces outnumbered and inexperienced – Dunbar, Berwick.

- Balliol captured at Montrose, imprisoned in Tower of London.

- Capture of John and 'honours' of Scotland marked effective end of separate Scottish kingdom.

- However, Balliol remained symbol, e.g. Wallace was fighting for Balliol in 1297–1304.

3. Explain the reasons why William Wallace was able to organise resistance to Edward I. **5**

Candidates must show a causal relationship between events.

Candidates must make a number of points that make the issue plain or clear, for example by showing connections between factors or causal relationships between ideas or events. These should be key reasons and may include theoretical ideas. There is no need for any evaluation or prioritising of these reasons.

Candidates may provide a number of straightforward reasons, a smaller number of developed reasons, or a combination of these.

Up to the total mark allocation for this question: 1 mark should be given for each accurate relevant point. A second mark should be given for any mark that is developed.

Possible reasons may include:

- Wallace the younger son of a Lanarkshire lord – not just fighting for his own claim.

- Wallace fighting for the restoration of John Balliol, the rightful king.

- Wallace led the fight in the South of Scotland.

- Wallace fought alongside several guardians, such as Bishop Wishart, James Stewart.

- Also a rebellion in the North, which joined with Wallace's rising.

- Showed skill and bravery at Stirling Bridge.

- Andrew Murray died at Stirling Bridge leaving Wallace as the hero of the victory.

- Embodied the spirit of resistance to Edward – restored hope of victory.

- Sole Guardian of the realm in 1298.

- Harrying of the North of England.

- Loss of authority following defeat at Falkirk – resignation as Guardian.

- His standard and memory used by Bruce to rally support after 1306 – showing the impact he had.

Source B

> Before committing such a crime in a church, Robert the Bruce had followed a cautious policy to protect his lands and power by supporting Edward I's rule in Scotland.
>
> It is hard to escape the conclusion that the murder of Comyn [led to] Bruce's seizure of the throne as he realised that his best chance of salvation lay in his becoming king, thereby drawing on the natural loyalty which attached to the cause of a legitimate monarch.

4. How fully does **Source B** explain why Bruce fought against Edward I and his son after 1306? (Use **Source B** and recall.)   **5**

Candidates must make an overall judgement about the extent to which the source provides a full description/explanation of a given event or development.

One mark will be given for each valid point interpreted from the source or each valid point of significant omission provided. The candidate can achieve up to 3 marks for their interpretation of the parts of the source they consider relevant in terms of the proposed question, where there is also at least one point of significant omission identified to imply a judgement has been made about the limitations of the source.

For full marks to be given each point needs to be discretely mentioned in terms of the question.

A maximum of 2 marks may be given for answers which refer only to the source.

Possible points which may be identified in the source include:

- Source suggests that Bruce's priority had always been to protect his lands and rights and this had sometimes led him to support Edward.

- Bruce had committed a significant crime by murdering Comyn in a church.

- His best chance of not being condemned for killing Comyn was to have himself crowned king.

- The murder of Comyn pushed Bruce into radical action when before he had been cautious.

Possible points of significant omission may include:

- Bruce's grandfather had been one of the claimants to the throne under the Great Cause.

- Until 1306 the Guardians supported the Kingship of John Balliol.

- Bruce had been the leading Scottish supporter of Edward's cause, but most lords switched sides at various times.

- Following the death of William Wallace (a leading supporter of Balliol) and Comyn, Bruce was now the main candidate to rule Scotland.

- Precise events and Bruce's motives in killing Comyn are in dispute.

- Wallace showed the possibility of resistance to English rule.

- Cost of the Scottish wars, Edward I's age and death in 1307 seemed an opportunity.

- 1306–1309 Bruce still had to deal with other rivals and supporters of the Comyns before he could be the sole leader of the patriotic cause against Edward II.

- In his military tactics Bruce continued to be cautious until 1314 – avoiding pitched battle.

Part E – The Era of the Great War, 1910–1928

Source A

> There were not enough infantry to take advantage of this huge hole in the German defences and the enemy soon began to recover and fight back. By evening many tanks had broken down – over a hundred from lack of petrol or engine failure and another sixty five from enemy gunfire, including sixteen knocked out by a single German field gun. All these tanks were now stranded in German territory and there were no reserves.

1. How fully does **Source A** describe the impact of tanks on war on the Western Front? (Use **Source A** and recall.) **5**

Candidates must make an overall judgement about the extent to which the source provides a full description/explanation of a given event or development.

One mark will be given for each valid point interpreted from the source or each valid point of significant omission provided. The candidate can achieve up to 3 marks for their interpretation of the parts of the source they consider relevant in terms of the proposed question, where there is also at least one point of significant omission identified to imply a judgement has been made about the limitations of the source.

For full marks to be given each point needs to be discretely mentioned in terms of the question.

Possible points which may be identified in the source include:

- Tanks were able to make a significant breech in enemy lines.

- Infantry were required to consolidate the gains made by tanks.

- Tanks were unreliable and broke down.

- Tanks were vulnerable to well directed artillery fire.

Possible points of significant omission may include:

- Initially tanks were used solely to protect small numbers of infantry as they advanced.

- Cambrai was the first large-scale use of tanks and it demonstrated their potential to break a stalemate.

- Later learned to use large numbers of tanks to overcome the high attrition rate.

- In early battles tanks held element of terror and surprise.

- Tanks got stuck in the mud and tracks came detached.

- Tanks had propaganda value at home in films and posters.

2. Describe the ways in which conscientious objectors were treated during the war.　　　　**5**

Candidates must make a number of relevant, factual points. These should be key points. The points do not need to be in any particular order. The candidate may provide a number of straightforward points or a smaller number of developed points, or a combination of these.

Up to the total mark allocation for this question: 1 mark should be given for each accurate relevant point of knowledge. A second mark should be given for any point that is developed.

Candidates can be credited in a number of ways up to a maximum of 5 marks. They may take different perspectives on the events and may describe a variety of different aspects of the events.

Possible points of knowledge may include:

- The main groups of conscientious objectors were religious, e.g. Quakers or Jehovah's witnesses, or political, e.g. socialists, other pacifists.

- Treatment of men not in uniform, e.g. white feathers, 'conchies' or C.O.s.

- Some lost jobs.

- Military service act – introduction of conscription in 1916, now legal process to objection – conscience clause.

- Two alternatives – contribute in other ways, e.g. ambulance drivers/stretcher bearers or non co-operation with war effort – absolutists.

- Military tribunal.

- No Conscription Fellowship – some charged under DORA – fines/prison.

Source B is from a letter written by Emmeline Pankhurst to a Scottish Suffragette on 10 January 1913.

Source B

My Dear Friend

The Prime Minister has announced that the Women's Amendments to the Manhood Suffrage Bill will shortly be discussed in Parliament. The WSPU has declined to call any truce on its militant activities on the strength of the Prime Minister's promise to discuss the issue of votes for women. There is no commitment from the government to get the act carried. We must continue to show our determination. Women have been disappointed in the past. We will fight on and cause as much public disorder as we can. The cause is a just cause and it will triumph.

3. Evaluate the usefulness of **Source B** as evidence of the reasons why women won the vote in 1918.

   5

   (You may want to comment on who wrote it, when they wrote it, why they wrote it, what they say or what has been missed out.)

Candidates must evaluate the extent to which a source is useful by commenting on evidence such as the author, type of source, purpose and timing, content and omission.

For a mark to be given, the candidate must identify an aspect of the source and make a comment which shows how this aspect of the source makes the source more or less useful.

Up to the total marks allocation for this question: a maximum of 4 marks can be given for evaluative comments relating to author, type of source, purpose and timing. A maximum of 2 marks may be given for evaluative comments relating to the content of the source. A maximum of 2 marks may be given for points of significant omission.

Candidates can be credited in a number of ways up to a maximum of 5 marks.

Candidates must make a judgement about the usefulness of the source and support this by making evaluative comments on identified aspects of the source.

One mark will be given for each relevant comment made, up to a maximum of 5 marks in total.

Examples of aspects of the source and relevant comments

Author: The leader of the Suffragette movement.
Comment: Useful because she has a good understanding of the methods being used to try to win the vote.

Type of source: A personal letter.
Comment: This is useful because it is not intended for publication so it is not conscious of publicity or propaganda.

Purpose: To communicate the need to continue the campaign and encourage the movement in Scotland.

Comment: This is useful because it shows how the WPSU operated, but also might be overly positive to encourage action.

Timing: 1913.

Comment: Before World War I, which had an impact on winning suffrage. Useful however because it shows setbacks before war intervened.

Content: Disappointment in the inability to win full backing of government for the Conciliation Bill, determination to continue militant campaign.

Comment: This is useful in that it suggests the difficulty of winning over parliamentary support, but confidence that it is the Suffragettes' militancy that has advanced their case and will bring victory.

Points of significant omission:

- With outbreak of war 18 months later the militant campaign was called off.

- Militant tactics had hardened the views of those who opposed votes for women.

- Work of women during the war helped to persuade MPs to pass a degree of female suffrage as part of the Parliament Act 1918.

- But the tactics of the Suffragettes had arguably helped to force MPs to take the case for female suffrage seriously.

4. Explain the reasons why heavy industry declined in Scotland after the First World War.   **5**

Candidates must show a causal relationship between events.

Candidates must make a number of points that make the issue plain or clear, for example by showing connections between factors or causal relationships between ideas or events. These should be key reasons and may include theoretical ideas. There is no need for any evaluation or prioritising of these reasons.

Candidates may provide a number of straightforward reasons, a smaller number of developed reasons, or a combination of these.

Up to the total mark allocation for this question: 1 mark should be given for each accurate relevant point. A second mark should be given for any point that is developed.

Possible reasons may include:

- Worldwide economic slump.

- Initially a boom, but ended quickly.

- Mining, shipbuilding, engineering hit especially hard by end of wartime orders.

- These industries especially important in Scotland.

- War had just delayed a decline that might have happened earlier due to challenge from German shipyards and American production.

- During war 14% of Scottish workers dependant on shipbuilding – £16m of orders.

- Jute production – competition plus industrial action led to rapid decline.

- Skilled workers had lost status during the war and wanted to reassert their privileged position over unskilled workers.

- Industrial problems 1919 – campaign to reduce unemployment by restricting the working week – strike accompanied by use of force by army and police.

- Railway production declined as efficiency initiative led to amalgamation of railway companies and centralisation in London.

SECTION 2 – BRITISH

Part A – The Creation of the Medieval Kingdoms, 1066–1406

Source A was written by Gerald of Wales about King Henry II in his book "*Concerning the instruction of a Prince*", which he wrote after Henry's death to explain what a good king was. He was a part of his court.

Source A

> He was a man of easy access and patient with those of lesser rank, flexible and witty, second to none in politeness ... Strenuous in warfare ... Very shrewd in civil life ... He was fierce towards those who remained untamed, but merciful towards the defeated, harsh to his servants, expansive towards strangers, spent generously in public, frugal [careful with money] in private ... Humble, an oppressor of the nobility and a condemner of the proud.

1. Evaluate the usefulness of **Source A** as evidence of Henry's kingship.   **6**

    (You may wish to comment on who wrote it, when they wrote it, why they wrote it, what they say or what has been missed out.)

Candidates must evaluate the extent to which a source is useful by commenting on evidence such as the author, type of source, purpose and timing, content and omission.

For a mark to be given, the candidate must identify an aspect of the source and make a comment which shows how this aspect of the source makes the source more or less useful.

Up to the total marks allocation for this question: a maximum of 4 marks can be given for evaluative comments relating to author, type of source, purpose and timing. A maximum of 2 marks may be given for evaluative comments relating to the content of the source. A maximum of 2 marks may be given for points of significant omission.

Candidates can be credited in a number of ways up to a maximum of 5 marks.

Candidates must make a judgement about the usefulness of the source and support this by making evaluative comments on identified aspects of the source.

One mark will be given for each relevant comment made, up to a maximum of 5 marks in total.

Examples of aspects of the source and relevant comments

Author: Gerald of Wales.
Comment: As a member of the court he would have known the king well, so quite useful.

Type of source: A history of the English court.
Comment: This was written to explain the qualities of a King, which makes it very useful.

Purpose: To give a portrait of Henry as King.
Comment: Useful as Henry's character reflected the nature of his kingship.

Timing: After Henry's death.
Comment: Likely to be reliable – no hope of favour or fear of retribution from the king.

Content: A positive portrait, suggests he was good to those who supported him, but would be harsh with those who opposed him and no respecter of rank in doing so.
Comment: Mostly useful as there is some balance in his praise of Henry – admits that he is harsh to his servants – but may reflect the bias of a supporter.

Points of significant omission

- Treatment of Becket might be reflected in the harshness towards servants, but perhaps this was also a loss of temper, which is not reflected in Gerald's portrait of Henry.

- Reflects the ideas of ideal kingship of the time, not so clear about how he governed his lands.

- Because a portrait of Henry's personality, does not reflect some of his lasting achievements as King such as the reforms to the legal system.

2. To what extent did monasteries become the most important branch of the medieval church? **8**

Candidates must make a judgement about the extent to which different factors contributed to an event or development, or its impact. They are required to provide a balanced account of the influence of different factors and to come to a reasoned conclusion based in the evidence presented.

Up to 5 marks are allocated for relevant points of knowledge used to address the question. One mark should be given for each relevant, key point of knowledge used to support a factor. If only one factor is presented, a maximum of 3 marks should be given for relevant points of knowledge.

Factors may include the spiritual, economic, social and political roles of the regular church, including the following:

- Regular church viewed as 'spiritual knights' fighting evil through prayer.

- Cut off from society often in remote areas.

- Nobility prepared to donate large sums.

- Social function as outlet for younger children of nobility/alternative to knighthood.

- Refuge for widows, unmarried women.

- Educational function – schools.

- Support for travellers, in times of famine, sickness.

- Political functions, e.g. advisors to kings.

- Feudal function – landowners, Abbots as barons.

- Innovative in wool industry, iron production, etc.

- Secular church in more contact with ordinary people, e.g. priests lived with ordinary people.

- Any other valid interpretation...

Up to 3 marks should be given for presenting the answer in a structured way, leading to a conclusion which addresses the question as follows:

One mark for the answer being presented in a structured way, with knowledge being organised in support of different factors.

One mark given for a valid judgement or overall conclusion.

One mark given for a reason being provided in support of the conclusion.

3. Explain the reasons why castles were built across Britain under Norman rule.   **6**

Candidates must show a causal relationship between events.

Candidates must make a number of points that make the issue plain or clear, for example by showing connections between factors or causal relationships between ideas or events. These should be key reasons and may include theoretical ideas. There is no need for any evaluation or prioritising of these reasons.

Candidates may provide a number of straightforward reasons, a smaller number of developed reasons, or a combination of these.

Up to the total mark allocation for this question: 1 mark should be given for each accurate relevant point. A second mark should be given for any mark that is developed.

Possible reasons may include:

- Normans needed to establish control by a small number of nobles, initially over a hostile population.

- Feudal system – lords granted a feu wanted to establish their area of control.

- Mott and Bailey castles built quickly with wood and earth.

- Prestige – visible sign of the lord's power.

- Law and order in local village and surrounding area – policing.

- Legal and administrative centre – manorial courts, dungeons.

- Stone castles a sign of the permanence of Norman rule.

- Castles on borders and in contentious areas, e.g. Edward I's castle building in Wales.

- Because Motte and Bailey castles were effective they were adopted by lords in Scotland – Anglo-Norman and Flemish lords also settled in Scotland.

Part E – The Making of Modern Britain, 1880–1951

1. To what extent did Liberal Welfare Reforms 1906–14 successfully address the problem of poverty in Britain in the early 20th century? **8**

Candidates must make a judgement about the extent to which different factors contributed to an event or development, or its impact. They are required to provide a balanced account of the influence of different factors and to come to a reasoned conclusion based in the evidence presented.

Up to 5 marks are allocated for relevant points of knowledge used to address the question. One mark should be given for each relevant, key point of knowledge used to support a factor. If only one factor is presented, a maximum of 3 marks should be given for relevant points of knowledge.

Factors might include issues of child poverty, old age, sickness and unavoidable unemployment to some extent as follows:

- New Liberalism move away from traditional laissez-faire towards an approach not blaming poor – led by Lloyd George, Churchill.

- Reflected findings of Seebohm Rowntree – his study in York was very influential.

- Address uncertainties outside control of the poor – particularly in childhood, while unemployed and in old age.

- Child poverty – Free School Meals – children's charter – protection against physical abuse, medical inspections: the use of schools to identify poverty.

- Old Age Pensions – restricted in scope, over 70s and focused on particular jobs, but principle of Government intervention to ensure savings for old age.

- Many measures permissive rather than compulsory, leaving decision to local authorities, so not completely moved away from laissez-faire approach.

- National Insurance Acts 1911 – provision of unemployment benefit, medical treatment and sick pay.

- Labour Exchanges established to help get unemployed back to work.

- Also some legal improvements for working conditions – eight-hour day for miners, half-day for shop workers.

- Any other valid interpretation...

Up to 3 marks should be given for presenting the answer in a structured way, leading to a conclusion which addresses the question as follows:

One mark for the answer being presented in a structured way, with knowledge being organised in support of different factors.

One mark given for a valid judgement or overall conclusion.

One mark given for a reason being provided in support of the conclusion.

2. Explain the reasons why attitudes towards poverty in Britain changed during the Second World War. **6**

Candidates must show a causal relationship between events.

Candidates must make a number of points that make the issue plain or clear, for example by showing connections between factors or causal relationships between ideas or events. These should be key reasons and may include theoretical ideas. There is no need for any evaluation or prioritising of these reasons.

Candidates may provide a number of straightforward reasons, a smaller number of developed reasons, or a combination of these.

Up to the total mark allocation for this question: 1 mark should be given for each accurate relevant point. A second mark should be given for any mark that is developed.

Possible reasons may include:

- Beveridge Report showed cross-party consensus towards activist approach to dealing with the 'giant' of poverty.

- During World War II total war had meant increased government intervention to win the war – some would see a war on poverty as similar.

- Breaking down of social barriers in the armed forces.

- Rationing during war supported by propaganda against spivs and hoarders – a fairer distribution of food and resources.

- The Blitz required rapid rebuilding with cheap housing – opportunity for a new start based on a more shared outlook.

- Spread of socialist ideas in the army. Also alliance with Communist Russia.

- Wish to never return to the conditions of the 1930s Great Depression and slide to war associated with Conservative ideas.

- The Great Depression caused by worldwide economic conditions rather than the fecklessness of individuals – reinforced trend of move away from laissez-faire individualism begun under the Liberals.

- Labour election victory a landslide.

Source A is from an editorial in the *Daily Sketch* from February 1948 and refers to Bevan's negotiations with doctors about pay and conditions in the new NHS.

Source A

> The State medical service is part of the Socialist plot to convert Great Britain into a National Socialist economy. The doctors' stand is the first effective revolt of the professional classes against Socialist tyranny. There is nothing that Bevan or any other Socialist can do about it in the shape of Hitlerian coercion.

3. Evaluate the usefulness of **Source A** as evidence of reasons for the introduction of the NHS in 1948. **6**

(You may want to comment on who wrote it, when they wrote it, why they wrote it, what they say or what has been missed out.)

Candidates must evaluate the extent to which a source is useful by commenting on evidence such as the author, type of source, purpose and timing, content and omission.

For a mark to be given, the candidate must identify an aspect of the source and make a comment which shows how this aspect of the source makes the source more or less useful.

Up to the total marks allocation for this question: a maximum of 4 marks can be given for evaluative comments relating to author, type of source, purpose and timing. A maximum of 2 marks may be given for evaluative comments relating to the content of the source. A maximum of 2 marks may be given for points of significant omission.

Candidates can be credited in a number of ways up to a maximum of 5 marks.

Candidates must make a judgement about the usefulness of the source and support this by making evaluative comments on identified aspects of the source.

One mark will be given for each relevant comment made, up to a maximum of 5 marks in total.

Examples of aspects of the source and relevant comments

Author: Newspaper editorial.
Comment: As it is an attempt by a popular newspaper to shape public opinion, this may make it useful, but not necessarily related to the reasons for the NHS being introduced.

Type of source: Popular newspaper.
Comment: The author may wish to reflect the views of their readers in order to sell papers, which ought to make it useful.

Purpose: Attempt to shape public opinion.
Comment: The exaggerated language suggests that their view of the NHS as a 'socialist plot' is not very credible.

Timing: Feb 1948.
Comment: At the point at which Bevan is trying to persuade doctors to support the NHS.

Content: Portraying government as Nazis and the doctors as heroic resistance.

Comment: This is quite a biased and not very accurate reflection of views towards the NHS, although it did reflect the observations of Churchill that Labour would require a Gestapo to introduce the NHS. Although some doctors were resistant because they might lose private income, many others were pleased to have a regular income. Identifying former members of the wartime coalition with Hitler and the National Socialists is exaggerated and undermines the usefulness of this source.

Points of significant omission:

- View did reflect the observations of Churchill that Labour would require a Gestapo to introduce the NHS.

- The Welfare Reforms were first put forward in the Beveridge Report, which was produced with support across the parties during the war.

- Although some doctors were resistant because they might lose private income, many others were pleased to have a regular income.

- In the end Bevan made concessions that allowed private practice for doctors. Suggested that income, rather than fear of a Nazi NHS, central to doctors' resistance.

- The fact that Labour won the 1945 election by a landslide despite Churchill's comments suggested that very few agreed with Churchill's or the *Daily Sketch's* view of Attlee's government.

SECTION 3 – EUROPEAN AND WORLD

Part A – The Cross and the Crescent: the Crusades, 1071–1192

Sources **A** and **B** are about the reasons why people went on the First Crusade.

Source **A** is an extract from Pope Urban II's sermon at Clermont in 1095.

Source A

> This land you inhabit is everywhere shut in by the sea, is surrounded by ranges of mountains and is overcrowded by your numbers ... This is why you devour and fight one another, make war and even kill one another ... Let all dissensions [arguments] be settled. Take the road to the Holy Sepulchre, rescue that land from a dreadful race and rule over it yourselves.

Source B

> The preachers foretold confidently that the New Jerusalem would appear on earth when the Old Jerusalem was restored to Christian ownership. They spoke of a golden land, a land of milk and honey, where the rewards to those who helped to regain the Holy City for Christ would be immense.

1. Compare the views of **Sources A** and **B** about why people went on the First Crusade. (Compare the sources overall and/or in detail.) **4**

Candidates can be credited in a number of ways up to a maximum of 4 marks.

Candidates must make direct comparisons between the two sources either overall or in detail. A simple comparison will indicate what points of detail or overall comparison they agree or disagree about and should be given 1 mark.

A developed comparison in detail or overall viewpoint should be given 2 marks.

Candidates may achieve full marks by making four simple points, two developed points or a combination of these.

Possible points of comparison may include:

Source A	Source B
Overall emphasizes the shortage of land for knights as a reason for knights to leave Europe for crusade.	Overall emphasizes preaching about the riches of the lands around Jerusalem as an incentive to go on Crusade.
Land shortages have led knights to fight amongst one another in Europe.	Preachers portray a land of peace and prosperity under Christian control (a new Jerusalem).

Source A	Source B
The source also includes an inspiring call to 'rescue' the holy places of Jerusalem from Turkish control.	There would be a direct material reward for those who helped to capture Jerusalem for the Pope.
The source offers the land-hungry knights of Europe the opportunity to have new lands of their own to rule over.	Preachers painted a picture of the lands around Jerusalem as rich and golden.

2. Describe the course of the People's Crusade.   **5**

Candidates must make a number of relevant, factual points. These should be key points. The points do not need to be in any particular order. The candidate may provide a number of straightforward points or a smaller number of developed points, or a combination of these.

Up to the total mark allocation for this question: 1 mark should be given for each accurate relevant point of knowledge. A second mark should be given for any point that is developed.

Candidates can be credited in a number of ways up to a maximum of 5 marks. They may take different perspectives on the events and may describe a variety of different aspects of the events.

Possible points of knowledge may include:

- Preaching of itinerant preachers following the Pope's sermon at Clermont in 1095.

- The enthusiastic response of those from all classes of European society and not just the knights, the Pope's intended audience.

- The leadership of Peter the Hermit.

- The poor provision of the crusade as it progressed through Europe having left following a poor harvest.

- Opportunistic attacks on the Jewish population in parts of Germany and Austria – condemned by the Pope.

- Clashes with Byzantine forces on the fringes of the Byzantine Empire.

- Reception of Alexius Comnenus in Constantinople – suspicion, not what the Emperor had expected when he asked for help from the Pope and had behaved badly when they entered his Empire.

- Difficulties in Anatolia – divisions and looting local villages.

- Defeat at the Battle of Dorylaneum (Civetot).

3. Explain the reasons for the fall of the Kingdom of Jerusalem to Saladin in 1187.   **5**

Candidates must show a causal relationship between events.

Candidates must make a number of points that make the issue plain or clear, for example by showing connections between factors or causal relationships between ideas or events. These should be key reasons and may include theoretical ideas. There is no need for any evaluation or prioritising of these reasons.

Candidates may provide a number of straightforward reasons, a smaller number of developed reasons, or a combination of these.

Up to the total mark allocation for this question: 1 mark should be given for each accurate relevant point. A second mark should be given for any mark that is developed.

Possible reasons may include:

- Saladin and the unification of Islamic nations under his leadership.

- Guy de Lusignan and divisions within Outremer – hawkish Templar and Hospitaller leaders versus Raymond of Tripoli hoping to extend truce with Saladin.

- Raynald de Chatillon attacks a caravan from Cairo to Damascus, breaking truce with Saladin.

- May 1187 Saladin's invasion of Galilee.

- Attack on Tiberius, a diversion and trap for the Christian forces – Guy, afraid to be accused of cowardice, fell into the trap.

- Cut off from water they were drawn into being wiped out at the Horns of Hattin.

- The Battle of Hattin – all knights of the Kingdom of Jerusalem unwisely drawn into battle against Saladin's army of 30,000 – his largest ever army.

- Most garrisons decimated, towns apart from Tyre fell to Saladin. Jerusalem fell after a two-week siege.

Source C describes Richard I towards the end of the Third Crusade.

Source C

During the winter, when Saladin had disbanded most of his forces, Richard took the army on an expedition into the hills. They got to within twelve miles of Jerusalem. But it was clear that even if they took the city, there was no way to hold it once Richard and his army had gone. If they entered Jerusalem and fulfilled their vows, few in his army would be inclined to stay. There were not enough Christian knights who wanted to live out their lives in the Holy Land. With the French King already departed and his brother plotting against him at home, Richard was looking for a way out.

4. How fully does **Source C** explain the problems facing Crusaders on the Third Crusade?   **6**

Candidates must make an overall judgement about the extent to which the source provides a full description/explanation of a given event or development.

One mark will be given for each valid point interpreted from the source or each valid point of significant omission provided. The candidate can achieve up to 3 marks for their interpretation of the parts of the source they consider relevant in terms of the proposed question, where there is also at least one point of significant omission identified to imply a judgement has been made about the limitations of the source.

For full marks to be given each point needs to be discretely mentioned in terms of the question.

Possible points which may be identified in the source include:

- Richard had the opportunity to capture Jerusalem during the Third Crusade but he chose not to until he had secured the coast and defences against Egypt.

- Richard and his army could not stay because of threats to his kingdom in England and France.

- Jerusalem could not be held by the knights who had come on Crusade because most of them wanted to return once they had fulfilled their oaths to recapture Jerusalem.

Possible points of significant omission may include:

- The crusade was divided between French troops under the Duke of Burgundy, whose loyalty was to the King of France, who had already returned, and those under Richard's command.

- He had also offended Leopold of Austria and his followers.

- By contrast Richard's massacre of prisoners at Acre had united Saladin's forces against him and made compromise very difficult.

- Although Saladin also found it difficult to keep his troops together, he could gather his forces again quickly if Richard left.

Part D – Hitler and Nazi Germany, 1919–1939

1. Explain the reasons why there was opposition to the Weimar Republic in the early 1920s.

5

Candidates must show a causal relationship between events.

Candidates must make a number of points that make the issue plain or clear, for example by showing connections between factors or causal relationships between ideas or events. These should be key reasons and may include theoretical ideas. There is no need for any evaluation or prioritising of these reasons.

Candidates may provide a number of straightforward reasons, a smaller number of developed reasons, or a combination of these.

Up to the total mark allocation for this question: 1 mark should be given for each accurate relevant point. A second mark should be given for any mark that is developed.

Possible reasons may include:

- The Armistice – the first act of the new government was to concede defeat in the war – this led to the myth of the 'dolstoss', the stab in the back, amongst army veterans.

- The Treaty of Versailles – the new government was forced to sign this 'Dictated Peace'. This was extremely unpopular and there was violence in the early years of the Weimar Republic. Included the assassination of negotiators at Versailles. Becoming democratic was supposed to make the allies treat Germany more sympathetically.

- There were many unemployed soldiers – once organised into militia (Freikorps) to defeat the Communist Spartacist uprising in January 1919, it was easy for them to be used by right-wing political groups – led to the Kapp Putsch in 1920 and formed part of the membership of the Nazis who tried to carry out the Putsch in Munich in 1923.

- The inspiration of the Communist Revolution in Russia had already led to the creation of revolutionary groups in August 1918 and the far left did not support the moderate socialism of Ebert.

- The establishment were not sympathetic to the new democratic regime and were lenient in punishing right-wing opposition, e.g. Kapp Putsch only stopped by workers going on strike as the government could not command troops. The judges gave heavier punishments to the strikers that had saved the government than to the putschists who had tried to overthrow it.

- Economic problems – the war had created huge debts and the economy had to be rebuilt. This was made worse by the impact of reparations, which the government tried to meet by printing money, which led to the French and Belgian occupation of the Ruhr, which in turn led to the crisis of hyperinflation. Those who had their savings wiped out would never fully trust the government again.

Sources A and **B** are about the impact of the Great Depression on German politics.

Source A

Before the crash, 1.25 million people were unemployed in Germany. By the end of 1930 the figure had reached nearly 4 million, 15.3 per cent of the population ... wages also fell and those with full-time work had to survive on lower incomes. Hitler, who was considered a fool in 1928 when he predicted economic disaster, was now seen in a different light.

Source B

The Depression helped Hitler by undermining [German] democracy. The Republic was governed by coalitions because of the nature of the voting system. The Economic crisis caused the coalition under Muller to fall apart in 1930. The next three Chancellors ... relied on the President's powers ... to rule by decree without the support of the Reichstag. In this undemocratic atmosphere Hitler was able to come to power through the back door.

2. Compare the views of **Sources A** and **B** about the impact of the Great Depression on German politics. (Compare the sources overall and/or in detail.)   **4**

Candidates must make direct comparisons between the two sources either overall or in detail.

A simple comparison will indicate what points of detail or overall comparison they agree or disagree about and should be given one mark. A developed comparison in detail or overall viewpoint should be given 2 marks.

Candidates may achieve full marks by making four simple points, two developed points or a combination of these.

Possible points of comparison may include:

Source A	Source B
Overall suggests that popular support helped Hitler into power.	Overall suggests that it was not popular support, but manipulation of the undemocratic atmosphere that let Hitler in 'the back door'.
Hitler was made to look more credible by the depression as he had appeared to predict it.	Hitler was made to look more credible by the depression because the other parties appeared unable to cope with it.
People were in distress and began to look to Hitler for a solution.	Democracy was undermined by the crisis as Chancellors began to rule undemocratically by decree.
Unemployment went up very significantly and those in work were also affected by that.	The system of proportional representation led to coalitions that allowed Hitler in.

3. Describe the treatment of minority groups in Germany by the Nazis in the 1930s. **5**

Candidates must make a number of relevant, factual points. These should be key points. The points do not need to be in any particular order. The candidate may provide a number of straightforward points or a smaller number of developed points, or a combination of these.

Up to the total mark allocation for this question: 1 mark should be given for each accurate relevant point of knowledge. A second mark should be given for any point that is developed.

Candidates can be credited in a number of ways up to a maximum of 5 marks. They may take different perspectives on the events and may describe a variety of different aspects of the events.

Possible points of knowledge may include:

- Nazi racial theories – the idea of the Aryan master race meant that minorities were not regarded as truly German.

- Amongst the 'undesirables' under Nazi ideology were Jews, Jehovah's Witnesses, gypsies, the disabled.

- In 1933 the SA led a boycott of Jewish businesses and burned Jewish books.

- Jewish people lost jobs in the professions and the army.

- There was a huge propaganda campaign against Jewish people as well as other 'undesirable' groups.

- The school curriculum emphasised a version of German society and history that excluded minority groups.

- 1935 Nuremburg Laws removed German citizenship from Jewish people and they were legally separated from non-Jewish people by laws relating to marriage and relationships.

- From 1935 Roma ('gypsies') were rounded up and put into camps.

- Around 400 black Germans were forcibly sterilised.

- Things relaxed a little during the Berlin Olympics 1936.

- From 1937 a speech by Hitler led to an acceleration of the persecution of Jewish people as Jewish people had a red 'J' stamped on their passports. In November 1938 Kristallnacht led to the murder or imprisonment of hundreds of Jewish Germans.

- Disabled Germans were stigmatised, taken from their families and many were murdered as a part of the Nazi 'euthanasia programme'.

In **Source C** Hitler explains what he expects of young German men.

Source C

My teaching is hard. Weakness has to be knocked out of them. In my [New Order] a youth will grow up before which the world will shrink back. A violently active dominating, intrepid, brutal youth – that is what I am after. Youth must be all those things. It must be indifferent to pain. There must be no weakness or tenderness in it. I want to see once more in its eyes the gleam of pride and independence of the beast of prey. Strong and handsome must my young men be. I will have them fully trained in all physical exercises. I intend to have an athletic youth – that is the first and the chief thing. In this way I shall eradicate the thousands of years of human domestication. Then I shall have in front of me the pure and noble natural material. With that I can create the new order.

4. How fully does **Source C** explain Nazi policies towards young people in the 1930s?
    (Use **Source C** and recall.)   **6**

Candidates must make an overall judgement about the extent to which the source provides a full description/explanation of a given event or development.

One mark will be given for each valid point interpreted from the source or each valid point of significant omission provided. The candidate can achieve up to 3 marks for their interpretation of the parts of the source they consider relevant in terms of the proposed question, where there is also at least one point of significant omission identified to imply a judgement has been made about the limitations of the source.

For full marks to be given each point needs to be discretely mentioned in terms of the question.

Possible points which may be identified in the source include:

- Hitler wanted young German men to be 'violently' active and tough so that the rest of the world would be intimidated by them.

- Hitler wanted to eliminate all tenderness from young men so that they should feel no sympathy for the weak.

- He does not want them domesticated, but like 'beasts' or birds of prey.

- They should become a 'New Order' unlike previous generations of Germans.

Possible points of significant omission may include:

- Hitler wants to prepare young men to be soldiers.

- The Hitler Youth and school curriculum encouraged physical education above all.

- Hitler says nothing about the role of young women in the Nazi state.

- Girls were also expected to do a lot physical education to be physically strong and healthy.

- Girls were encouraged to be domestic, not to go out to do paid work, but to have as many German children as possible.

- During the 1930s it became increasingly difficult to opt out of the Nazi vision of youth as the school curriculum was changed and non-Nazi teachers sacked to support this vision, while peer pressure to join the Hitler Youth was strong.

- Many young Germans were inspired by the Nazi vision and joined the Hitler Youth.

- The Nazis encouraged the generation gap and propaganda encouraged young Germans to betray their parents if they stepped out of line at home. Parents were afraid to speak out or to stop their children going to the Hitler Youth.

- However, many young Germans did become disenchanted with the Hitler Youth.

- The Nazi vision did not apply to all Germans as Jewish children, those from other minorities, the disabled and homosexual young people were shunned or persecuted.

SECTION 1 – SCOTTISH

Part A – Mary Queen of Scots and the Scottish Reformation, 1542–1587

Source A is about the consequences of the Rough Wooing.

Source A

> The costs of the war are hard to assess. Government and society stood up well to seven years of garrisoning, forced quarter and violence. The Church suffered the most, but the effects were mixed: the occupation had greatly accelerated the spread of Protestant literature, which would later be blamed ... as the principal cause of the spread of heresy (reformation ideas), but collaboration with the English had also helped to drive the movement underground.

1. How fully does **Source A** explain the impact of the "Rough Wooing" on Scotland?   **5**

Candidates must make an overall judgement about the extent to which the source provides a full description/explanation of a given event or development.

One mark will be given for each valid point interpreted from the source or each valid point of significant omission provided. The candidate can achieve up to 3 marks for their interpretation of the parts of the source they consider relevant in terms of the proposed question, where there is also at least one point of significant omission identified to imply a judgement has been made about the limitations of the source.

For full marks to be given each point needs to be discretely mentioned in terms of the question.

Possible points which may be identified in the source include:

- For the most part Scots were unaffected by the Rough Wooing.

- There was little long-term economic damage to Scotland.

- The Reformation was driven underground in the short term as Protestant Scots seen as potential enemies within.

- In the long term the Rough Wooing may have encouraged Protestantism in Scotland.

Possible points of significant omission may include:

- The burning of Leith and Dunbar.

- Military defeats at Ancrum Moor and Pinkie Cleugh.

- Scots split, e.g. Borderers allying with Henry VIII's forces on Black Saturday.

- Scots' objections to the Greenwich Treaties, e.g. having to break Auld Alliance.

- English unable to impose authority beyond the garrisons that they established.

- Huge drain on the English treasury meant threat of future invasion receded.

- Mary Queen of Scots sent to France – strengthened Auld Alliance in the short term.

2. Describe the role of John Knox in the Reformation in Scotland. **5**

Candidates must make a number of relevant, factual points. These should be key points. The points do not need to be in any particular order. The candidate may provide a number of straightforward points or a smaller number of developed points, or a combination of these.

Up to the total mark allocation for this question: 1 mark should be given for each accurate relevant point of knowledge. A second mark should be given for any point that is developed.

Candidates can be credited in a number of ways up to a maximum of 5 marks. They may take different perspectives on the events and may describe a variety of different aspects of the events.

Possible points of knowledge may include:

- Protestantism in Scotland before Knox – Cardinal Beaton's persecution Hamilton, resistance of Wishart.

- Knox born around 1510 in Haddington – later trained as a Catholic priest.

- Knox involved in siege of St Andrew's Castle and exiled.

- Unbending opposition to Catholicism.

- Reputation as a Protestant preacher in exile around Europe.

- Return to Scotland 1559 – small and previously suppressed Protestant community energised by accession of Elizabeth in England.

- Protestants included powerful nobility – established Lords of the Congregation led by James Stewart.

- Knox gave leadership through preaching – whipping up iconoclastic crowds.

- Scottish Parliament banned celebration of the Catholic Mass.

- Preaching against Mary Queen of Scots and personally in one-to-one meetings.

- Helped further by poor marriages made by Mary.

- Died 1572 but influence felt in power of Kirk, especially after the reign of James VI.

In **Source B** Mary Queen of Scots tried to communicate a message to Queen Elizabeth explaining her actions after the murder of Darnley.

Source B

> I am more upset than anyone at the tragic death of my husband: if my subjects had allowed me to act and if they had given me free use of my authority as Queen, I would have punished those responsible. I had no knowledge of who those people were and none of my subjects told me that those who are now held to be guilty of carrying out this crime were the ones most responsible for committing it; if they had done, I would certainly not have acted as I have up to now. I believe that I have done nothing except at the advice of the nobility of the realm.

3. Evaluate the usefulness of **Source B** as evidence of Mary Queen of Scots actions at the time of the murder of Darnley. **5**

Candidates must evaluate the extent to which a source is useful by commenting on evidence such as the author, type of source, purpose and timing, content and omission.

For a mark to be given, the candidate must identify an aspect of the source and make a comment which shows how this aspect of the source makes the source more or less useful.

Up to the total marks allocation for this question: a maximum of 4 marks can be given for evaluative comments relating to author, type of source, purpose and timing. A maximum of 2 marks may be given for evaluative comments relating to the content of the source. A maximum of 2 marks may be given for points of significant omission.

Candidates can be credited in a number of ways up to a maximum of 5 marks.

Candidates must make a judgement about the usefulness of the source and support this by making evaluative comments on identified aspects of the source.

One mark will be given for each relevant comment made, up to a maximum of 5 marks in total.

Examples of aspects of the source and relevant comments

Author: Mary Queen of Scots.
Comment: Useful because she will be the person best placed to know what her actions were.

Type of source: A personal letter about her motives and actions to Elizabeth I.
Comment: This should be useful because it is an accurate reflection of the version of events that Mary wishes to communicate.

Purpose: To present a justification of her actions in the face of accusations of involvement in Darnley's murder.
Comment: She has every incentive to lie about the real course of events.

Timing: Shortly after the murder of Darnley.
Comment: Mary accused of Darnley's murder and Scottish nobility want to put her on trial. This makes the source less useful as, with her life and throne at stake, and hoping for help from Elizabeth, she will not tell the whole truth.

Content: Blames the nobility for preventing her exercising her authority and giving her bad advice. Claims to have known nothing about those who committed the murder.

Comment: This is useful because it shows Mary's desperation.

Points of significant omission:

Mary does not address her more suspicious actions:

- Marrying Bothwell.

- Finding herself at another engagement when Darnley was killed.

- Darnley's role in the murder of Rizzio.

4. Explain the reasons why Mary Queen of Scots was executed in 1587.   5

Candidates must show a causal relationship between events

Candidates must make a number of points that make the issue plain or clear, for example by showing connections between factors or causal relationships between ideas or events. These should be key reasons and may include theoretical ideas. There is no need for any evaluation or prioritising of these reasons.

Candidates may provide a number of straightforward reasons, a smaller number of developed reasons, or a combination of these.

Up to the total mark allocation for this question: 1 mark should be given for each accurate relevant point. A second mark should be given for any mark that is developed.

Possible reasons may include:

- Ambiguous position of Mary following Elizabeth's dismissal of casket letters.

- Mary's claim to the throne but apparent innocence of the crime against Darnley.

- Throckmorton and Parry plots show that Mary is a threat.

- Decline in power of Mary's supporters in Scotland.

- Mary's involvement with Babington plot against Elizabeth's life.

- Position of Catholics in England and hopes for a Catholic monarch.

- Role of Sir Francis Walsingham in entrapping Mary.

- Elizabeth's concerns about killing a fellow monarch.

- Suggestion of a quiet execution dismissed.

- Burley and the Council have Elizabeth's signed orders for execution sent to Fotheringay without her knowledge.

Part D – Migration and Empire, 1830–1939

1. Explain the reasons why people from Ireland and Europe arrived in Scotland in the 19th century.   **5**

Candidates must show a causal relationship between events.

Candidates must make a number of points that make the issue plain or clear, for example by showing connections between factors or causal relationships between ideas or events. These should be key reasons and may include theoretical ideas. There is no need for any evaluation or prioritising of these reasons.

Candidates may provide a number of straightforward reasons, a smaller number of developed reasons, or a combination of these.

Up to the total mark allocation for this question: 1 mark should be given for each accurate relevant point. A second mark should be given for any mark that is developed.

Possible reasons may include:

- Push and pull factors.

- Early immigration agricultural labour – harvest.

- Poverty and land shortage.

- The Irish Potato Famine – 90% increase in Irish population in Scotland.

- Industrial development in West of Scotland.

- Large amount of unskilled labour – coal mining, docks.

- Decline in Catholic emigration after 1870s replaced by Ulster Protestant immigration.

- Family links to previous immigrants.

- 1890s–1914 immigration from Southern and Eastern Europe – mainly male.

- Poverty in Southern Italy.

- Eastern European coal mining experience and industrial skills and demand for labour in Central Scotland.

- Opportunities in tailoring and restaurant trade.

- Largest single group of incomers English migrants – particularly important in the establishment of industries, e.g. cotton – skills and experience – opportunities for entrepreneurs.

- Professionals, e.g. in Edinburgh.

Source A is about migration from the Highlands and Lowlands of Scotland in the 19th Century.

Source A

> There was undoubtedly coercion (use of force), with the many in arrears over their rent being offered a choice of a free passage or eviction from their crofts. Between 1841 and 1861 the population of the West Coast above Ardnamurchan and the Inner and Outer Hebrides went down by a third. After that, though emigration continued apace, it was largely from the Lowlands, driven not by destitution (extreme poverty), but by the prospect of better opportunities.

2. How fully does **Source A** explain the reasons for migration from Scotland in the 19th century? **5**

Candidates must make an overall judgement about the extent to which the source provides a full description/explanation of a given event or development.

One mark will be given for each valid point interpreted from the source or each valid point of significant omission provided. The candidate can achieve up to 3 marks for their interpretation of the parts of the source they consider relevant in terms of the proposed question, where there is also at least one point of significant omission identified to imply a judgement has been made about the limitations of the source.

For full marks to be given each point needs to be discretely mentioned in terms of the question.

Possible points which may be identified in the source include:

*   Use of force.

*   Poverty and inability to pay rent.

*   Incentives to emigrate from the Highlands and Islands.

*   Lowland emigration influenced more by 'pull' than by 'push' factors.

Possible points of significant omission may include:

*   Rapid rise in population.

*   Development of new technologies and patterns of agricultural practice reduced need for labour on the land.

*   An extension of the migration within Scotland, sometimes temporary, that had been a feature for decades.

*   Ease and speed of transport abroad, e.g. steam boats.

*   Opportunities opened up by English-speaking Empire and Commonwealth.

*   More favourable climate in some destinations.

*   The opening up of lands in Canada and America for settlement.

Source B is an account of Irish sugar-workers in Greenock, 1836 from a Report on the State of the Irish Poor in Great Britain, Parliamentary Papers.

Source B

> Mr Thomas Fairrie, sugar manufacturer, of Greenock [stated] 'If it was not for the Irish, we should be obliged to import Germans, as is done in London. The Scotch will not work in sugar-houses; the heat drives them away in the first fortnight. If it was not for the Irish, we should be forced to give up trade; and the same applies to every sugar-house in town. This is a well-known fact. Germans would be our only resource, and we could not readily get them. Highlanders would not do the work'.

3. Evaluate the usefulness of **Source B** as evidence of the reaction to Irish immigrants in Scotland.   **5**

   (You may want to comment on who wrote it, when they wrote it, why they wrote it, what they say or what has been missed out.)

Candidates must evaluate the extent to which a source is useful by commenting on evidence such as the author, type of source, purpose and timing, content and omission.

For a mark to be given, the candidate must identify an aspect of the source and make a comment which shows how this aspect of the source makes the source more or less useful.

Up to the total marks allocation for this question: a maximum of 4 marks can be given for evaluative comments relating to author, type of source, purpose and timing. A maximum of 2 marks may be given for evaluative comments relating to the content of the source. A maximum of 2 marks may be given for points of significant omission.

Candidates can be credited in a number of ways up to a maximum of 5 marks.

Candidates must make a judgement about the usefulness of the source and support this by making evaluative comments on identified aspects of the source.

One mark will be given for each relevant comment made, up to a maximum of 5 marks in total.

Examples of aspects of the source and relevant comments

Author: Witness in a Parliamentary investigation. A factory owner.
Comment:

- Very useful as he is speaking to an official body, knows about why Irish labourers might be employed.

- An eyewitness who was involved.

Type of source: Parliamentary report.
Comment: Useful because the witness' views are reliably reported, factual.

Purpose: An attempt to get objective information about Irish immigration.
Comment: Useful because there is no reason for the report to show bias.

Timing: 1836.
Comment: Useful only to an extent because at this point Irish immigration is limited compared to the numbers after the famine.

Content: Irish workers are more likely than migrants from the Highlands to work reliably in the uncomfortable conditions of the sugar houses and easier to obtain than German workers.
Comment: Useful in explaining why the Irish were employed, but only a narrow view of Scottish reaction to Irish immigration.

Points of significant omission:

- Irish arrived in much greater numbers from 1840s onwards.

- Does not reflect negative cultural response to Irish immigration – particularly sectarian concern.

- Does not comment on how Highlanders and other Scots might feel about willingness of Irish to take jobs in poorer conditions and lower wages.

4. Describe the role played by Scots in the development of the British Empire between 1830 and 1939.   **5**

Candidates must make a number of relevant, factual points. These should be key points. The points do not need to be in any particular order. The candidate may provide a number of straightforward points or a smaller number of developed points, or a combination of these.

Up to the total mark allocation for this question: 1 mark should be given for each accurate relevant point of knowledge. A second mark should be given for any point that is developed.

Candidates can be credited in a number of ways up to a maximum of 5 marks. They may take different perspectives on the events and may describe a variety of different aspects of the events.

Possible points of knowledge may include:

- Union in 1707 gave Scots access to the largest trading area in the world and they made good use of it.

- Tobacco and fur trade dominated by Scots in America (i.e. in 1830 onwards, Canada).

- Railways, banking, jute, etc. trading in India.

- Shipping and frozen goods.

- Sheep farming New Zealand and Australia.

- Administration of India.

- Establishment of schools.

- Protestant missionaries.

- Colonisation.

- Oppression of native peoples.

- Examples of individuals rising to prominence:
  - Colin Campbell
  - Thomas Lipton
  - David Livingstone.

- The usefulness of Scottish cliques in building business connections.

- Role of Scottish regiments in establishing and imposing control in largest Empire in history.

SECTION 2 – BRITISH

Part C – War of the Three Kingdoms, 1603–1651

Source A is from a speech given by King James VI/I to Parliament, March 1610.

Source A

> The state of monarchy is the supreme thing upon earth; for kings are not only God's lieutenants on earth and sit upon God's throne, but even by God himself are called gods. There are three things that illustrate the nature of monarchy: one from the Bible, the others from policy and philosophy. In the Scriptures kings are called gods and so their power can be compared to the divine power. Kings are also compared to the fathers of families, for the king truly is father of his country, the political father of his people. And lastly, kings are compared to the head of this microcosm (small model) of the body of man.

1. Evaluate the usefulness of **Source B** as evidence of the nature of Royal Authority 1603–25. **6**

    (You may want to comment on who wrote it, when they wrote it, why they wrote it, what they say or what has been missed out.)

Candidates must evaluate the extent to which a source is useful by commenting on evidence such as the author, type of source, purpose and timing, content and omission.

For a mark to be given, the candidate must identify an aspect of the source and make a comment which shows how this aspect of the source makes the source more or less useful.

Up to the total marks allocation for this question: a maximum of 4 marks can be given for evaluative comments relating to author, type of source, purpose and timing. A maximum of 2 marks may be given for evaluative comments relating to the content of the source. A maximum of 2 marks may be given for points of significant omission.

Candidates can be credited in a number of ways up to a maximum of 5 marks.

Candidates must make a judgement about the usefulness of the source and support this by making evaluative comments on identified aspects of the source.

One mark will be given for each relevant comment made, up to a maximum of 5 marks in total.

Examples of aspects of the source and relevant comments

Author: King James VI.
Comment: Useful, as key person to the assertion of Royal Authority. Has been King in Scotland for a long time before becoming King in England.

Type of source: A speech to Parliament.
Comment: Useful, as this is what he wants to be understood as the status of the King.

Purpose: Explaining his status to Parliament.
Comment:

- Less useful as this may not be the reality.

- But James' hope/belief based on his experience in Scotland.

Timing: 1610.
Comment: Still relatively early in his reign in England.

Content:

- Emphasises the supremacy of the monarch over all other parts of the kingdom.

- Compares himself as King to God.

- Compares himself as King to the head of a body.

- Compares himself as King to the father of a family, with subjects as children.

- Argument from religion and reason.
Comment: As his reign went on his attitude towards the role of the King would be a recurring point of dispute with subjects, particularly in Parliament.

Points of significant omission:

- James had clashed with this Parliament over monopolies and it would be dismissed the following year.

- 1611–1621 Parliament only sat for eight weeks (addled Parliament 1614) because James did not think it had the right to discuss issues of Royal finances or favourites – showing again that James' view of Royal Authority was not universally shared.

- In 1621 the Parliament wanted to discuss its own authority and rights in relation to the Crown.

- In 1624 James had to call Parliament again to raise finance for war with Spain and again Parliament wanted to discuss matters James thought were not its business – James was arguably finding it increasingly difficult to exercise power and authority in the way he stated in the source.

2. To what extent did challenges to Royal Authority in Scotland cause the outbreak of war between Charles I and English Parliamentarians in 1641? **8**

Candidates must make a judgement about the extent to which different factors contributed to an event or development, or its impact. They are required to provide a balanced account of the influence of different factors and to come to a reasoned conclusion based in the evidence presented.

Up to 5 marks are allocated for relevant points of knowledge used to address the question. One mark should be given for each relevant, key point of knowledge used to support a factor. If only one factor is presented, a maximum of 3 marks should be given for relevant points of knowledge.

Factors mentioned might include: money, religion, Charles, Parliament and foreign affairs, all of which might be related by the candidate directly or indirectly to events in Scotland leading up to 1642.

Relevant points of knowledge including:

- Parliament had used restricted finance to make Charles consult it, e.g. granting of Tonnage and Poundage, Petition of Right. Charles resented this and tried to rule without Parliament.

- Charles had to use innovative means of taxation – resentment in England and Scotland.

- 11 Years' Tyranny brought to an end and crisis initiated by need to pay for war with Scots: Short Parliament called.

- Lack of finance for war led to defeat for the King's army, paid off Scots Covenanters threatening to invade northern England £850 per day – led directly to Charles calling the Long Parliament – left with little room for manoeuvre.

- Archbishop Laud tried to impose English Prayer Book on Scotland, Anglican dress, threatened introduction of Bishops/abolition of presbyteries – led to St Giles riot and the Covenant 1638.

- English Parliamentarians sympathised with the Scots – saw the prayer book as too Catholic – Laud put on trial.

- 30 Years' War was a religious conflict in which Protestantism appeared under threat – fear in England and Scotland that treatment of Protestants on the continent might be replicated.

- Charles' Catholic wife and his appointment of High Church Laud as Archbishop of Canterbury.

- Irish Catholic rebellion brought issues to a head – cost, religion, suspicion of Charles' wish to rule without Parliament.

- Charles' belief in Divine Right and inflexibility – made Parliament suspicious of him and led to his rash policies, e.g. the introduction of a new prayer book; his failed attempt to arrest Members of Parliament.

- Deteriorating relations between Charles and his Scottish subjects turned underlying issues from discontent into direct confrontation and war.

Up to 3 marks should be given for presenting the answer in a structured way, leading to a conclusion which addresses the question as follows:

One mark for the answer being presented in a structured way, with knowledge being organised in support of different factors.

One mark given for a valid judgement or overall conclusion.

One mark given for a reason being provided in support of the conclusion.

3. Explain the reasons why King Charles I was executed in 1649.   **6**

Candidates must show a causal relationship between events.

Candidates must make a number of points that make the issue plain or clear, for example by showing connections between factors or causal relationships between ideas or events. These should be key reasons and may include theoretical ideas. There is no need for any evaluation or prioritising of these reasons.

Candidates may provide a number of straightforward reasons, a smaller number of developed reasons, or a combination of these.

Up to the total mark allocation for this question: 1 mark should be given for each accurate relevant point.

A second mark should be given for any reason that is developed.

Candidates may receive full marks by providing five straightforward reasons, three developed reasons or a combination of these.

Possible reasons may include:

- Views of Cromwell – judgement of God on Charles, "the man against which The Lord hath witnessed".

- Charles was not sincere in his negotiations with Parliament for a compromise.

- Secret intrigues with Irish rebels continuing even after the failure of his negotiations with the Scots.

- Charles was the 'Man of Blood' blamed by the regicides for causing the Second Civil War.

- In the eyes of the regicides, Charles refused to recognise the judgement of God in his defeat in 1646.

- Legal justification in Roman Law, justifying overthrow of a tyrant.

- Most parliamentarians opposed trial of the King, but Pride's Purge left only the 'Rump' who supported it, though many reluctantly.

- Only 58 of 135 nominees to the court signed the verdict.

- Charles refused to defend himself or recognise the court – given the lack of support for the trial he could have more effectively defended himself. He would not go quietly.

- However, control and influence of the army under Cromwell and Ireton determined outcome.

Part D – Changing Britain, 1760–1900

1. Explain the reasons for housing problems in British cities in the first half of the 19th century.

6

Candidates must show a causal relationship between events.

Candidates must make a number of points that make the issue plain or clear, for example by showing connections between factors or causal relationships between ideas or events.

These should be key reasons and may include theoretical ideas. There is no need for any evaluation or prioritising of these reasons.

Candidates may provide a number of straightforward reasons, a smaller number of developed reasons, or a combination of these.

Up to the total mark allocation for this question: 1 mark should be given for each accurate relevant point. A second mark should be given for any mark that is developed.

Possible reasons may include:

- Rapid urbanisation – lack of urban planning and overcrowding.

- Local government had difficulty adjusting to the demands of change.

- Population of Britain and Ireland 16.3 million in 1801, 24 million in 1831.

- Poor sanitation, ventilation and development of slums.

- Epidemics of diseases such as Cholera, tuberculosis, typhus and typhoid directly linked to poor sanitation.

- Lack of knowledge of causes of disease – John Snow's work on cholera in London in 1831 began to make a difference.

- Poor food quality – adulteration and poor storage.

- Although much less overcrowding, in the countryside houses of the poor were very basic and often damp. However sanitation less of a problem so life expectancy for labourers in the countryside in 1840s twice that in the towns and cities.

Source A is from an article in the *Scottish Railway Gazette* for April 1845.

Source A

> Railways will mean that all parts of the country will become more opened up. Land in the interior will, by a system of cheap and rapid transport for manure and farm produce, become almost as valuable as land on the coast. The man of business can as easily join his family at a distance of 10 or 12 miles as could formerly be done at 2 or 3 miles.

2. Evaluate the usefulness of **Source A** as evidence of the impact of railways on Britain.   **6**

(You may want to comment on who wrote it, when they wrote it, why they wrote it, what they say or what has been missed out.)

Candidates must evaluate the extent to which a source is useful by commenting on evidence such as the author, type of source, purpose and timing, content and omission.

For a mark to be given, the candidate must identify an aspect of the source and make a comment which shows how this aspect of the source makes the source more or less useful.

Up to the total marks allocation for this question: a maximum of 4 marks can be given for evaluative comments relating to author, type of source, purpose and timing. A maximum of 2 marks may be given for evaluative comments relating to the content of the source. A maximum of 2 marks may be given for points of significant omission.

Candidates can be credited in a number of ways up to a maximum of 5 marks.

Candidates must make a judgement about the usefulness of the source and support this by making evaluative comments on identified aspects of the source.

One mark will be given for each relevant comment made, up to a maximum of 5 marks in total.

Examples of aspects of the source and relevant comments

Author: *Scottish Railway Gazette.*
Comment:

- Useful because knowledgeable.

- But may be biased as pro-railway.

Type of source: A specialist journal.
Comment: Knowledgeable, but biased (see above).

Purpose: To comment on the effect railways are having on British life.
Comment: That they feel a need to comment reflects remarkable impression of railways on those witnessing its expansion.

Timing: 1845.
Comment:

- Contemporary.

- Well into period of most rapid expansion in railway building, so useful as railways have already made a difference.

Content:

- Predicting the future impact rather than discussing existing impact.

- However, many of these predictions broadly correct as commuting became feasible and land in areas previously cheap became valuable.

- Businesses, trade and towns growing up around railways.

Comment:

- This makes it less useful in theory as this is speculative rather than factual in tone.

- But turns out to be reasonably accurate.

Points of significant omission:

- The diet of people living in towns and cities improved and became more varied.

- Boost to engineering, iron and coal industries.

- Postal and communications impact.

- The nationalisation of politics.

- The growth of seaside resorts.

- Increase in immigration to help build railways (e.g. Irish 'Navvies').

- The decline of canals.

- There was a negative environmental impact in some areas.

3. To what extent was Parliamentary Reform in the 19th century brought about by the actions of radical protesters?   **8**

Candidates must make a judgement about the extent to which different factors contributed to an event or development, or its impact. They are required to provide a balanced account of the influence of different factors and to come to a reasoned conclusion based in the evidence presented.

Up to 5 marks are allocated for relevant points of knowledge used to address the question. One mark should be given for each relevant, key point of knowledge used to support a factor. If only one factor is presented, a maximum of 3 marks should be given for relevant points of knowledge.

Factors mentioned might include: radical parliamentary reformers, Chartists, party leaders and social changes in education and organisation.

Relevant points of knowledge including:

- In the 20 years after the French Revolution there were a series of radical campaigns for parliamentary reform – no significant concessions were made.

- The 1832 Reform Act was not mainly caused by radical protests, although there were some.

- 1832 was followed by increased campaigning for reform under the Chartists, culminating in the Kennington Petition 1848 – however this made no difference to parliamentary reform at the time.

- The wealthier Anti-Corn Law League was much more successful than the Chartist movement.

- However, five of the six points of the Charter did become law eventually.

- A lot of radicals joined the new Liberal Party from the 1860s and pushed for reform from within.

- Liberals wanted to include more of the newly prosperous people in Britain in the system.

- Some of the strange aspects of the old system increasingly seemed irrational to Liberal MPs.

- The extension of free education from the 1870s persuaded more MPs to support reform.

- Political concerns – politicians like Disraeli and Gladstone were concerned about beating the other side rather than the arguments or campaigns of radicals.

- Although it did not truly take off until the 1900s, the campaign for votes for women was begun by radical campaigners, such as John Stuart Mill, who proposed an amendment to the 1867 Reform Act.

- Initially campaigning for votes for women was peaceful, emphasising women's readiness to vote rather than protest.

Up to 3 marks should be given for presenting the answer in a structured way, leading to a conclusion which addresses the question as follows:

One mark for the answer being presented in a structured way, with knowledge being organised in support of different factors.

One mark given for a valid judgement or overall conclusion.

One mark given for a reason being provided in support of the conclusion.

SECTION 3 – EUROPEAN AND WORLD

Part E – Red Flag: Lenin and the Russian Revolution, 1894–1921

1. Describe the problems facing Russian agriculture and industry before 1905.   **5**

Candidates must make a number of relevant, factual points. These should be key points. The points do not need to be in any particular order. The candidate may provide a number of straightforward points or a smaller number of developed points, or a combination of these.

Up to the total mark allocation for this question: 1 mark should be given for each accurate relevant point of knowledge. A second mark should be given for any point that is developed.

Candidates can be credited in a number of ways up to a maximum of 5 marks. They may take different perspectives on the events and may describe a variety of different aspects of the events.

Possible points of knowledge may include:

- Over 80% of the population of the Russian Empire were peasants.

- Peasants had been freed from serfdom in the 1861 Emancipation Proclamation, but resented that they now had to pay Redemption to the landlords in compensation.

- Peasant life was based around the Mir, the village commune, in which village elders determined the distribution of strips of land and resources.

- Peasant farming was conservative and mainly subsistence, so that only limited amounts of surplus was sold.

- Most of the profit and innovation in agriculture came from the lands of the nobility, which peasants still worked, but no longer as serfs.

- Industry had taken off rapidly from the late 1880s onwards through the investment of the government and foreign investors given incentives by the government.

- The government invested mainly in railways and heavy industry, particularly by building the Trans-Siberian railway. They hoped this would create the engineering and iron, steel and coal mining basis for rapid Industrialisation.

- Government investment was paid for through heavy taxation of the peasantry, which put greater strain upon them.

- Industrialisation was rapid but concentrated in very small parts of European Russia – mainly around St Petersburg and Moscow.

- Although there were lots of different kinds of factories, the very large ones were the most productive. These put workers into barrack-like accommodation and treated them harshly, which created discontent.

Sources A and **B** describe the Tsar's government of Russia between 1905 and 1914.

Source A

The Tsar felt forced to promise a kind of constitution in October 1905. The Duma was very weak: it could not make laws, the Council of Ministers was selected by the Tsar and elections to the Duma were rigged to ensure that the nobility had the strongest representation and the more radical liberals were excluded. Even so, the Tsar resented sharing his ancient autocratic powers with anybody else. Having stepped away from the old ways of ruling, he tried to avoid having to deal with the Duma, cutting back its powers even more when he had the chance.

Source B

The half-hearted concessions that the Tsar made in 1905 to share power with society represented by political parties neither made the regime more popular with the opposition nor raised his prestige with the people at large. They could not understand how a proper ruler could allow himself to be openly criticised by another government institution. His divine right to rule depended on his ability to rule forcefully. Nicholas II fell not because he was hated, but because he was held in contempt.

2. Compare the views of **Sources A** and **B** about the Tsar's government of Russia between 1905 and 1914. (Compare the sources overall and/or in detail.) **4**

Candidates can be credited in a number of ways up to a maximum of 4 marks.

Candidates must make direct comparisons between the two sources either overall or in detail. A simple comparison will indicate what points of detail or overall comparison they agree or disagree about and should be given 1 mark.

A developed comparison in detail or overall viewpoint should be given 2 marks.

Candidates may achieve full marks by making four simple points, two developed points or a combination of these.

Possible points of comparison may include:

Source A	Source B
Overall criticises the Tsar for taking power back from the Duma and leaving it weak.	Overall criticises the Tsar for not acting more strongly against the Duma/for making concessions at all.
Political parties openly disagreed with him.	People could not understand how the supreme ruler of the Russian Empire would allow criticism from another government institution.
The Tsar had an ancient autocratic power that he resented sharing.	His divinely ordained power relied on his ability to rule forcefully.
Having taken a step towards democracy, the Tsar then tried to undermine it.	The Duma neither made him more popular nor raised his prestige.

Source C is about Order No. 1 issued on 1 March 1917.

Source C

> The Petrograd Soviet effectively controlled transport and communications and workers and soldiers looked to it for leadership. There was therefore 'dual power' because, while the Soviet was happy for the Provisional Government of the Duma to take control of the government, the Soviet itself had many of the reins of power. On 1 March it issued Army Order No 1: no one should do what the Provisional Government said unless the Soviet agreed.

3. How fully does **Source C** explain the failure of the Provisional Government in 1917? (Use **Source C** and recall.) **6**

Candidates must make an overall judgement about the extent to which the source provides a full description/explanation of a given event or development.

One mark will be given for each valid point interpreted from the source or each valid point of significant omission provided. The candidate can achieve up to 3 marks for their interpretation of the parts of the source they consider relevant in terms of the proposed question, where there is also at least one point of significant omission identified to imply a judgement has been made about the limitations of the source.

For full marks to be given each point needs to be discretely mentioned in terms of the question.

Possible points which may be identified in the source include:

- The problem of dual power – the Provisional Government depended from the start on the support of the Petrograd Soviet to get anything done – obey orders only in as far as they do not contradict the Soviet.

- Army discipline – the Provisional Government believed that the war with Germany must be won, but Order No. 1 made the army more difficult to organise.

- Fighting on the front line difficult when there are two lines of command – officers and Soviet Committees.

- The Soviet was supported by workers and soldiers who looked to it for leadership. The Provisional Government would not have any unless it called elections to a Constituent Assembly.

Possible points which are not identified in the source include:

- The members of the Petrograd Soviet were opposed to anything other than a defensive war, while members of the Provisional Government wanted to win the war with Germany.

- The Liberals in the Provisional Government put off calling elections because they knew that they would lose.

- Publication of the Miliukov Note, showing that the Provisional Government wanted to fight on led to a crisis in the relationship between the Soviet and Provisional Government.

- The economic situation in the cities got worse.

- In July 1917 Kerensky's crushing of the Bolshevik uprising made it look as if the Provisional Government could survive a further revolution.

- Army generals felt unsure about the Provisional Government.

- The Kornilov Coup put the Bolsheviks in a strong position to overthrow the Provisional Government under the slogan "All power to the Soviets".

- As discipline broke down - soldiers were beginning to desert.

- The Tsar's government had disappeared suddenly without the time to establish something in its place.

- When the Bolsheviks carried out their Coup d'état in the name of the Soviets, no one came to the Provisional Government's rescue.

4. Explain the reasons why the Bolsheviks defeated the White forces in the Civil War.   **5**

Candidates must show a causal relationship between events.

Candidates must make a number of points that make the issue plain or clear, for example by showing connections between factors or causal relationships between ideas or events. These should be key reasons and may include theoretical ideas. There is no need for any evaluation or prioritising of these reasons.

Candidates may provide a number of straightforward reasons, a smaller number of developed reasons, or a combination of these.

Up to the total mark allocation for this question: 1 mark should be given for each accurate relevant point. A second mark should be given for any mark that is developed.

Possible reasons may include:

- The Reds controlled the central area of Russia around Moscow and Petrograd – this meant that they always had good internal lines of communication, a ready supply of troops and access to industry to produce arms and other equipment required to win the war.

- The Reds had determined leaders – in particular Lenin and Trotsky ensured unity, pragmatism and good use of propaganda – imposed strict discipline, used ex-Tsarist officers, sometimes under duress and Trotsky travelled around the front line exhorting troops to energetic resistance.

- The Reds represented both Russia and the Revolution. Those who did not want the Tsar back or who resented the intervention of America, Britain, France and Japan in Russian affairs preferred the Reds to the Whites.

- The Whites had poor communications and had different aims – at the beginning, for example, they included Social Revolutionaries, Mensheviks and Tsarist generals who all had different visions for the future of Russia. Later different generals vied to be 'Supreme Leader'.

- There were atrocities on both sides, but White officers often attempted to return land and property to landlords by force, leading to greater resentment against them.

- White efforts were not well co-ordinated.

- The allies were half-hearted in their intervention as the First World War was over.

Part H – Appeasement and the Road to War, 1918–1939

Source A is about the Treaty of Versailles, signed in June 1918.

Source A

> Germany was given two choices: either to sign the Treaty or to be invaded by the Allies.
>
> They signed the Treaty as in reality they had no choice. When the ceremony was over, Clemenceau went out into the gardens of Versailles and said, "it is a beautiful day".
>
> The Treaty seemed to satisfy the "Big Three" as in their eyes it was a just peace as it kept Germany weak yet strong enough to stop the spread of communism; kept the French border with Germany safe from another German attack and created the organisation, the League of Nations, that would end warfare throughout the world.
>
> However, it left a mood of anger throughout Germany as it was felt that as a nation Germany had been unfairly treated.

1. How fully does **Source A** explain the consequences of the Treaty of Versailles?
   (Use **Source A** and recall.)   **6**

Candidates must make an overall judgement about the extent to which the source provides a full description/explanation of a given event or development.

One mark will be given for each valid point interpreted from the source or each valid point of significant omission provided. The candidate can achieve up to 3 marks for their interpretation of the parts of the source they consider relevant in terms of the proposed question, where there is also at least one point of significant omission identified to imply a judgement has been made about the limitations of the source.

For full marks to be given each point needs to be discretely mentioned in terms of the question.

Possible points which may be identified in the source include:

- The source suggests that the Big Three were satisfied with the balance of the treaty.

- Germany should remain strong enough to resist the spread of Communism from Russia, France protected from invasion and a League established to keep the peace.

- The Treaty was a 'Dictated Peace' or Diktat, as the source suggests the German delegation had no say over the content of the treaty.

- The Treaty was a source of anger and resentment in Germany.

Possible points which are not identified in the source include:

- In reality Clemenceau would rather that Germany had been left even weaker so it could not threaten France again.

- The League of Nations was fatally weakened by the absence of the USA and the lack of an armed force to support its resolutions.

- The reparations clauses made worse the several years of crisis that followed in Germany, leading to hyperinflation in 1923 and making Germany more vulnerable to the Wall Street Crash later.

- Germany lost much of its armed forces, was divided by the Polish corridor and lost all of its colonies.

- Making the newly democratic government of Germany sign what was seen as a blatantly unfair treaty fundamentally undermined the democratic constitution of Germany.

- The Treaty was used as reason for right wing opposition groups such as the Nazis to attack the democratic government.

- Although greatly weakened, Germany was in fact strong enough to become a threat to Europe once again, including an invasion of France.

2. Explain the reasons why the Nazis adopted an aggressive foreign policy in the 1930s.   **5**

Candidates must show a causal relationship between events.

Candidates must make a number of points that make the issue plain or clear, for example by showing connections between factors or causal relationships between ideas or events. These should be key reasons and may include theoretical ideas. There is no need for any evaluation or prioritising of these reasons.

Candidates may provide a number of straightforward reasons, a smaller number of developed reasons, or a combination of these.

Up to the total mark allocation for this question: 1 mark should be given for each accurate relevant point. A second mark should be given for any mark that is developed.

Possible reasons may include:

- Adolf Hitler became Chancellor of Germany in 1933 promising to make Germany great again – his book *Mein Kampf* suggested that this would mean invading other countries to create Lebensraum and destroying the Treaty of Versailles.

- Japan in Manchuria had shown that the League of Nations would not take tough action against aggressors.

- Initially Germany was isolated so Germany's foreign policy appeared more reasonable – withdrew from the Disarmament Conference because other countries would not disarm, withdrew from the League because it was associated with the Treaty of Versailles and signed a non-aggression pact with Poland.

- In 1934 tested the water with support for Austrian Nazis, but backed down in the face of Italian threats.

- Turning points in 1935 and 1936 led to a much more aggressive approach – Anglo-German Naval Agreement gave permission to Germany to rearm, while the Italian invasion of Abyssinia broke the Stresa Front of Britain, France and Italy against German rearmament.

- The French Government was weak and often disagreed with British policy. Increasingly it was the British that felt isolated.

- 1936 re-occupation of the Rhineland tested the water again, this time showing that the Treaty of Versailles could be overthrown through limited military action. The British in particular seemed willing to renegotiate the terms of the Treaty of Versailles.

- 1936–39 the Spanish Civil War brought Hitler and Mussolini closer, while dividing those opposed to Hitler: Britain, France and the USSR – Germany was no longer isolated and Hitler felt able to proceed with the Anschluss with Austria.

- The Hossbach Memorandum shows that by 1938 German foreign policy was being driven by the need to create 'Lebensraum' by 1940 as the re-armament programme was 'overheating' the German economy.

- The idea that Hitler could achieve his aims of overthrowing Versailles and creating Lebensraum without a major war was further encouraged by the British policy of appeasement that sought to negotiate concessions to Germany – this led to the increasing aggression in Germany's approach to Czechoslovakia and Poland in 1938–39.

Sources B and **C** are about the reasons why Britain adopted a policy of Appeasement towards Germany in the 1930s.

Source B

The Government was concerned with the weakness of its armed forces, notably the lack of home defences, especially against the bomber. There had been widespread disarmament in the 1920s; there were no troops immediately available to mount a challenge.

The heads of Britain's armed forces – Chiefs of Staff – consistently warned Chamberlain that Britain was too weak to fight. Alongside this Nazi propaganda encouraged Britain and France to believe that Germany's forces were a lot stronger than they really were.

Source C

> Appeasement was a reasonable response to the problems facing Britain in the 1930s. The British Empire stretched around almost a quarter of the globe and despite the strains of defending such an extensive area, dominion governments expressed limited enthusiasm for helping the mother country if drawn into a major conflict in Europe. The cost of defending an overseas empire with a strong navy conflicted with the demands of defending Britain from aerial threats and the possibility of a land war in Europe. Meanwhile there remained a strong pacifist mood in British society that politicians could not ignore.

3. Compare the views of **Sources B** and **C** about the reasons for the British policy of Appeasement. (Compare the sources overall and/or in detail.) **4**

Candidates can be credited in a number of ways up to a maximum of 4 marks.

Candidates must make direct comparisons between the two sources either overall or in detail. A simple comparison will indicate what points of detail or overall comparison they agree or disagree about and should be given 1 mark. A developed comparison in detail or overall viewpoint should be given 2 marks. Candidates may achieve full marks by making four simple points, two developed points or a combination of these.

Possible points of comparison may include:

Source B	Source C
Overall this source is mainly concerned about the weakness of the British armed forces.	Overall, this source is mainly concerned with the difficulty of defending the British Empire.
The Chiefs of Staff were telling the British Government that forces we're too weak to fight.	Source C suggests that Appeasement was a reasonable policy given the problems that Britain had to face in the 1930s.
There was a particular concern about the impact that German air power might have on Britain.	What was required to defend an overseas empire – a strong navy, was not the same as that required to defend Britain against aerial attack.
The threat from Germany's armed forces was exaggerated by propaganda and greatly overestimated by Britain's leadership.	Dominion governments seemed unlikely to help in the defence of Britain in a war with Germany.

4. Describe the attempts to address German demands over Czechoslovakia in 1938. **5**

Candidates must make a number of relevant, factual points. These should be key points. The points do not need to be in any particular order. The candidate may provide a number of straightforward points or a smaller number of developed points, or a combination of these.

Up to the total mark allocation for this question: 1 mark should be given for each accurate relevant point of knowledge. A second mark should be given for any point that is developed.

Candidates can be credited in a number of ways up to a maximum of 5 marks. They may take different perspectives on the events and may describe a variety of different aspects of the events.

Possible points of knowledge may include:

- France and the Soviet Union guaranteed that they would honour treaty agreement to defend Czechoslovakia.

- Henlein and the Karlsbad Decrees demanded autonomy for German areas.

- A firm line in support of Czechoslovakia had helped avert crisis in May 1938.

- Britain and France did not want to be pushed into war by the Czechs, and Hitler did not want to be seen to have backed down again.

- Runciman tried to negotiate during summer 1938, but Sudeten Nazis increased their demands.

- Chamberlain proposed to meet and then did meet Hitler at Berchtesgaden.

- At Berchtesgaden Chamberlain agreed to persuade Czechs to give up the Sudetenland on the basis of self-determination.

- Chamberlain persuaded the French and forced the Czechs to accept the Berchtesgaden proposal.

- At Bad Godesburg Chamberlain found that Hitler wanted to increase his demands to expel non-German speakers for Sudetenland and take over almost immediately. War looked inevitable.

- An exchange of letters between Hitler and Chamberlain and Mussolini's intervention led to a new conference at Munich on 29 September.

- A four-power conference led to the Munich Agreement in which Germany was to take over the Sudetenland in stages. The Czechs were not consulted.

Chamberlain got Hitler to sign separately a declaration that Britain and Germany would continue to negotiate and not go to war again. Chamberlain returned to Britain to a hero's welcome.

SECTION 1 – SCOTTISH

Part C – The Treaty of Union, 1689–1715

Source A is about the Worcester Affair, which was a part of the increasing tensions between Scotland and England in the years before the Act of Union.

Source A

> The seizure of the Annandale increased ill feeling in Scotland. In July 1704 an English ship, the Worcester, anchored at Leith. The directors of the Company of Scotland, thinking she was an East India Company ship, seized her in exchange for the Annandale. Suspicions were aroused that she had played a part in the loss of another Company ship, the Speedy Return, off the coast of Africa in1703. In September 1704, Captain Green and the crew of the Worcester were arrested and charged with piracy and murder. The Admiralty Court jury consisted of Edinburgh merchants and sea captains, some of whom were shareholders in the Company of Scotland. In March 1705, despite a lack of evidence against them, Green and two of his men were sentenced to death.

1. How fully does **Source A** explain the reasons for tension between England and Scotland before 1707? (Use **Source A** and recall.)   **5**

Candidates must make an overall judgement about the extent to which the source provides a full description/explanation of a given event or development.

One mark will be given for each valid point interpreted from the source or each valid point of significant omission provided. The candidate can achieve up to 3 marks for their interpretation of the parts of the source they consider relevant in terms of the proposed question, where there is also at least one point of significant omission identified to imply a judgement has been made about the limitations of the source.

For full marks to be given each point needs to be discretely mentioned in terms of the question.

Possible points which may be mentioned in the source include:

*   Refers to the seizure of the *Annandale* and trading tensions between Scotland and England over the East India Company.

*   England excluding Scotland from her growing empire was a cause of tension.

*   The execution of the Captain of the Worcester and two of his men was carried out on very little evidence.

*   Describes the atmosphere of outrage in Scotland especially amongst traders and those associated with the Company of Scotland.

Possible points of significant omission include:

- The Darien Scheme – its failure and England's role in ensuring it failed.

- The Act Anent Peace and War – Scots Parliament's declaration that they would follow their own foreign policy as England became drawn into the War of the Spanish Succession.

- The Security Act – Scottish Parliament threatened to choose a different monarch from England if their trading rights were not restored.

- The Alien Act – English Parliament threatened to treat Scots as Aliens with no property rights in England – threatened those with property with confiscation.

Source B is by John Erskine, Earl of Mar, Secretary of State in Scotland, writing a letter to the Earl of Godolphin, Lord Treasurer of England, 16 September, 1706.

Source B

> When I came here first, there were very few people in town, so I went to my country house and stayed till last Saturday. I talked with a great many and found most of them against the Union, but when I told them what it was and the advantages they did not expect such terms, so that most of them were mightily softened and some entirely converted.

2. Evaluate the usefulness of **Source B** as evidence of how Scots felt about the Act of Union.   5

   (You may want to comment on who wrote it, when they wrote it, why they wrote it, what they say or what has been missed out.)

Candidates must evaluate the extent to which a source is useful by commenting on evidence such as the author, type of source, purpose and timing, content and omission.

For a mark to be given, the candidate must identify an aspect of the source and make a comment which shows how this aspect of the source makes the source more or less useful.

Up to the total marks allocation for this question: a maximum of 4 marks can be given for evaluative comments relating to author, type of source, purpose and timing. A maximum of 2 marks may be given for evaluative comments relating to the content of the source. A maximum of 2 marks may be given for points of significant omission.

Candidates can be credited in a number of ways up to a maximum of 5 marks.

Candidates must make a judgement about the usefulness of the source and support this by making evaluative comments on identified aspects of the source.

One mark will be given for each relevant comment made, up to a maximum of 5 marks in total.

Examples of aspects of the source and relevant comments

Author: Secretary of State for Scotland, Earl Mar.
Comment: A member of the Government before the Act of Union makes it useful because of his general knowledge of the situation.

Type of source: A private letter.
Comment: Not concerned about publicity – useful as he would be expected to give a truthful assessment of the position to a government colleague.

Timing: Before the passage of the Union.
Comment: Reflects people's views at the prospect of Union rather than the reality – so less useful.

Purpose: To give a colleague an informed opinion about the views of Scots towards the prospects of Union.
Comment: He at least is trying to be truthful, but may be tempted to put a more positive spin on what he hears.

Content: Found most Scots to be initially against the Union, but quickly won round once they knew more about what it involved.
Comment:

- Useful as it suggested that at least amongst those the Earl of Mar knew there may have been suspicion and lack of knowledge about the Union and many Scots could be won over by it.

- You might expect that those in his circle would be among the better informed, so might suggest that knowledge of what the Union might mean in practice was limited in general.

Points of significant omission:

- Jacobite success in the election of 1703.

- The possibility of Union appeared very quickly without time for widespread debate.

- No election to gauge popularity – suggest pro-Union party knew it was not widely popular in Scotland.

- Riots and petitions and protest meetings in around a quarter of the shires and a third of the burghs of Scotland.

3. Describe the role of the Duke of Hamilton in the passage of the Treaty of Union.   **5**

Candidates must make a number of relevant, factual points. These should be key points. The points do not need to be in any particular order. The candidate may provide a number of straightforward points or a smaller number of developed points, or a combination of these.

Up to the total mark allocation for this question: 1 mark should be given for each accurate relevant point of knowledge. A second mark should be given for any point that is developed.

Candidates can be credited in a number of ways up to a maximum of 5 marks. They may take different perspectives on the events and may describe a variety of different aspects of the events.

Possible points of knowledge may include:

- Leader of the Country Party.

- Key figure opposing Union.

- Speech on 1 September 1705 called for Union Commissioners to be nominated by the Queen, not by Parliament.

- Key to victory of pro-Union Court Party as opposition would get no representation on the Commission.

- Seen as a betrayal of his own side – left the chamber – nomination by the Queen approved by just eight votes.

- Later rewarded with a Dukedom, Ambassador to Paris and other honours as well as strong suspicion of bribery.

- Went back to supporting anti-Union stance.

- Union may not have happened without his action.

4. Explain the reasons for the Jacobite rebellion of 1715. **5**

Candidates must show a causal relationship between events.

Candidates must make a number of points that make the issue plain or clear, for example by showing connections between factors or causal relationships between ideas or events. These should be key reasons and may include theoretical ideas. There is no need for any evaluation or prioritising of these reasons.

Candidates may provide a number of straightforward reasons, a smaller number of developed reasons, or a combination of these.

Up to the total mark allocation for this question: 1 mark should be given for each accurate relevant point. A second mark should be given for any mark that is developed.

Possible reasons may include:

- Lack of economic benefits for most Scots under the Union.

- Failed attempt at landing by Jacobite James VIII backed by French 1708.

- Narrow defeat of motion to end the Union in House of Lords 1714 showed disappointment.

- James VIII wrote to Mar urging him to raise an army.

- Earl of Mar had originally voted for the Union.

- Death of Queen Anne and the Act of Succession.

- Unpopularity of the Hanovarians in Scotland – reminder of how Union has been imposed.

- Scots divided about the restoration of the Stewarts – mainly along religious lines.

- Support for Earl of Mar mainly North of the Tay – Episcopalian rather than Presbyterian, so more sympathetic to Catholic Jacobite cause (James Head of the Church).

- Argyll's rule and the actions of the Campbells created resentment from other clans.

- Mar raised the old royal standard at Castletown near Braemar 6 Sept 1715.

Part E – The Era of the Great War, 1910–1928

Source A is about recruitment to the British Army during World War One.

Source A

> Usually the rush of Scots to join the army in 1914 is put down to enthusiasm and patriotic fervour. Following the call from Parliament for 100 000 men to join the British Expeditionary Force, the army was overwhelmed with 750 000 volunteers in the first six weeks. By January over a million had joined up. While defence of 'King and Country' was important to many, others were pushed to join up by the wish to escape unemployment or through the encouragement of employers or others, not to mention the peer pressure created by the formation of "Pals' Battalions" in towns, villages and workplaces.

1. How fully does **Source A** explain the motives of those volunteering for the army in the first year of World War One? (Use **Source A** and recall.) **5**

Candidates must make an overall judgement about the extent to which the source provides a full description/explanation of a given event or development.

One mark will be given for each valid point interpreted from the source or each valid point of significant omission provided. The candidate can achieve up to 3 marks for their interpretation of the parts of the source they consider relevant in terms of the proposed question, where there is also at least one point of significant omission identified to imply a judgement has been made about the limitations of the source.

For full marks to be given each point needs to be discretely (separately) mentioned in terms of the question.

Possible points which may be mentioned in the source include:

- Many joined out of patriotism – to defend King and Country.

- Peer pressure/Pals Battalions not wanting to let your friends down when whole villages or workplaces joining up.

- Unemployment and low pay made the army attractive to many.

- Some employers supported recruitment drives.

Possible points of omission include:

- Use of propaganda to make young men feel guilty.

- Graphic portrayal of atrocities committed by German troops.

- White feathers handed out to young men not in uniform to show that others thought they were cowards.

- Travel unusual in 1914 – adventure.

- Heroic images of war from books and newspapers before 1914.

- Belief that it would all be "over by Christmas".

- Discussion of unemployment in particular areas of Scotland.

2. Explain the reasons why Scottish industries were important to the war effort in World War One. **5**

Candidates must show a causal relationship between events.

Candidates must make a number of points that make the issue plain or clear, for example by showing connections between factors or causal relationships between ideas or events. These should be key reasons and may include theoretical ideas. There is no need for any evaluation or prioritising of these reasons.

Candidates may provide a number of straightforward reasons, a smaller number of developed reasons, or a combination of these.

Up to the total mark allocation for this question: 1 mark should be given for each accurate relevant point. A second mark should be given for any mark that is developed.

Possible reasons may include:

- The war required industries already strong in Scotland – shipbuilding, textiles, engineering and paper production, for example.

- Expertise and skills available for mass production of a variety of related products

- Skilled workers exempt from national service.

- Shipbuilders came under direct control of the admiralty to prioritise new wartime needs.

- In the West of Scotland in particular there was an expansion in war industries.

- Firms began to diversify into new areas to meet the needs of war, e.g. shipbuilders Beardmores produced aircraft and artillery as well as ships.

- John Brown, shipbuilder produced tanks from 1916.

- 90% of plate armour came from Glasgow.

- North British Rubber Company in Edinburgh and North British Locomotive Company in Springburn in demand.

- Also new purpose-built munitions factories such as large one in Gretna employing 9000 women and 5000 men.

- Albion Motor works famous for lorry making, North British engine works biggest manufacturer of diesel engines for ships.

3. Describe the impact of the Defence of the Realm Act on people living in Scotland. **5**

Candidates must make a number of relevant, factual points. These should be key points. The points do not need to be in any particular order. The candidate may provide a number of straightforward points or a smaller number of developed points, or a combination of these.

Up to the total mark allocation for this question: 1 mark should be given for each accurate relevant point of knowledge. A second mark should be given for any point that is developed.

Candidates can be credited in a number of ways up to a maximum of 5 marks. They may take different perspectives on the events and may describe a variety of different aspects of the events.

Possible points of knowledge may include:

- Original Act passed in 1914, but amended throughout the war.

- Measures to prevent spying – bans on use of binoculars, kite flying, lighting bonfires, fireworks, melting down gold, spreading rumours relating to the military, discussion of military matters in public.

- Ban on trespassing on railway lines or bridges to prevent sabotage.

- Measures to control information – censorship of newspapers.

- Measures to increase production and efficiency at work – licensing laws, British Summer Time, beer watered down, rounds in pubs banned.

- Measures to control production for military purposes – government could take over any factory or workplace and requisition any land it wanted.

- Measures to reduce consumption of foodstuffs – ban on feeding bread to livestock.

- Unprecedented powers for a government over civilian population in Britain.

Source B is from the pamphlet "Manifesto of the Joint Strike Committee, Glasgow: a call to British Labour", 31 January 1919.

Source B

> Dastardly attempt to smash Trade Unionism
>
> The Joint Committee. ... Initiated the movement for a Forty Hours week with a view to absorbing the unemployed. A strike for this object began on 27th January. This has the support of Trades Unionists all over the British Isles. ... (On Friday 31st January) The bludgeon attack on the strikers .... was deliberately ordered by the officers and was unprovoked. The attack was sheer brutality by the police to satisfy the lust of the masters for broken skulls.

4. Evaluate the usefulness of **Source B** as evidence of disturbances on Clydeside.   **5**

   (You may want to comment on who wrote it, when they wrote it, why they wrote it, what they say or what has been missed out.)

Candidates must evaluate the extent to which a source is useful by commenting on evidence such as the author, type of source, purpose and timing, content and omission.

For a mark to be given, the candidate must identify an aspect of the source and make a comment which shows how this aspect of the source makes the source more or less useful.

Up to the total marks allocation for this question: a maximum of 4 marks can be given for evaluative comments relating to author, type of source, purpose and timing. A maximum of 2 marks may be given for evaluative comments relating to the content of the source. A maximum of 2 marks may be given for points of significant omission.

Candidates can be credited in a number of ways up to a maximum of 5 marks.

Candidates must make a judgement about the usefulness of the source and support this by making evaluative comments on identified aspects of the source.

One mark will be given for each relevant comment made, up to a maximum of 5 marks in total.

Examples of aspects of the source and relevant comments

Author: Organisers of strike action in Glasgow.
Comment: Useful as it was written by direct witnesses to what happened in January 1919.

Type of source: A public and published manifesto concerning the disturbances.
Comment: May be less useful as evidence of the disturbances as it is designed to influence others and get a response.

Purpose: To state the Trade Unionists' version of events and call for support for their cause from across Britain.
Comment: Useful as it gives a version of events different to that given by the police or employers, but may be open to exaggeration or bias.

Timing: Two days after the events described.
Comment: Useful because the events are fresh in their minds, but possibly less so because it may be influenced by passion and anger.

Content: Outlines the reasonable motives behind strike action and the unprovoked brutality of the police in suppressing it as well as the guilt of employers in instigating it.
Comment: Useful because it tells a little of the background to unrest as well as what happened on Bloody Friday itself.

Points of significant omission:

* CWC loose coalition of shop stewards and others had won concessions during war time.

* Bluff and double bluff – no barricades or violence planned, but 'drastic action' threatened.

* Some unions did not support the action – separate negotiations with ASE official engineers union.

* Fear of Bolshevik or Spartacist uprising.

* Troops and artillery deployed.

SECTION 2 – BRITISH

Part C – The Atlantic Slave Trade, 1770–1807

1. Explain the impact of the Triangular Trade on the British economy.   **6**

Candidates must make a number of points that make the issue plain or clear, for example by showing connections between factors or causal relationships between ideas or events. These should be key reasons and may include theoretical ideas. There is no need for any evaluation or prioritising of these reasons.

Candidates may provide a number of straightforward reasons, a smaller number of developed reasons, or a combination of these.

Up to the total mark allocation for this question: 1 mark should be given for each accurate relevant point. A second mark should be given for any mark that is developed.

Possible reasons may include:

- Triangular trade involved the export of British goods from British ports to Africa, and the import of produce from the Caribbean and America into British ports.

- The cities most directly involved were Liverpool, Bristol and London, which benefitted substantially from this profitable trade.

- Liverpool profited by £300 000 each year from the trade and other major ports each made about the same.

- Glasgow imported over half of all of the tobacco imported into Europe.

- A large amount of employment created in building and equipping ships with sails, rope, provisions.

- Textiles and clothing for slaves produced in British mills.

- Processing of tobacco, sugar, etc. in factories in Britain.

- Glasgow grew from small and poor town to become the second city of the Empire.

- Any other valid points.

Source A is a court record from Dominica, part of the British Colony in the Leeward Islands, January 1814.

Source A

1814 Jan[uar]y 15	John Pierre	Mr Grano	Co[ur]t Martial	Attempting to return to the Runaways with Provisions & having been runaway 2 Months	To be hanged	Hanged: Head cut off & put on a Pole. Body hanged on a Gibbet, 16 Jan[uar]y 1814
	Sarah	ditto	ditto	ditto	To receive 50 lashes	Pardoned & released 30th Jan[uar]y
	Hetty, Penny & Placide	ditto	ditto	ditto	To receive 40 lashes each	Received 40 lashes each & returned to owner's att[ention] 22nd Jan[uar]y
28	Joseph	Mr Dubocq	ditto	supplying Runaways with salt & with provisions	Not guilty	Discharged
	Pierre	Mr Polus Estate	ditto	Encouraging the Neg[roe]s upon that estates who had absconded to stay away	To receive 100 lashes & to be worked in chains 6 months	Rec[eived] 100 lashes & died in Jail 6 april
	Charles	Mr Bonnjean	ditto	Being runaway near 17 months	ditto	Rec[eived] 100 lashes

2. Evaluate the usefulness of **Source A** in explaining the treatment of slaves on Caribbean plantations. **6**

(You may want to comment on who wrote it, when they wrote it, why they wrote it, what they say or what has been missed out.)

Candidates must evaluate the extent to which a source is useful by commenting on evidence such as the author, type of source, purpose and timing, content and omission.

For a mark to be given, the candidate must identify an aspect of the source and make a comment which shows how this aspect of the source makes the source more or less useful.

Up to the total marks allocation for this question: a maximum of 4 marks can be given for evaluative comments relating to author, type of source, purpose and timing. A maximum of 2 marks may be given for evaluative comments relating to the content of the source. A maximum of 2 marks may be given for points of significant omission.

Candidates can be credited in a number of ways up to a maximum of 5 marks.

Candidates must make a judgement about the usefulness of the source and support this by making evaluative comments on identified aspects of the source.

One mark will be given for each relevant comment made, up to a maximum of 5 marks in total.

Examples of aspects of the source and relevant comments

Author: Official court records.
Comment: A factual record of punishments.

Type of source: Court record.
Comment: Factual record, so very useful.

Purpose: Record sentences, crimes and punishments.
Comment: Very useful as it's reliable and contains specific detailed information.

Timing: 1814.
Comment: Useful – primary, from the height of the use of slave labour in the Caribbean.

Content: Shows slaves were punished extremely harshly for mutinies, running away and aiding runaways.
Comment: Very useful as it not only shows the harsh methods used to keep slaves in order but also persistence and extent of resistance to slavery.

Points of significant omission:

- Limited portrayal of daily life on the plantations.

- Slaves had no rights on plantations and could be lashed without trial.

- The harsh working conditions of field slaves punishing in themselves.

- High death rate due to heat, poor nutrition, brutality and disease, only gradually improved by the Amelioration Act 1798.

3. To what extent can the abolition of the slave trade be explained by the actions of abolitionist campaigners in Parliament? **8**

Candidates must make a judgement about the extent to which different factors contributed to an event or development, or its impact. They are required to provide a balanced account of the influence of different factors and to come to a reasoned conclusion based in the evidence presented.

Up to 5 marks are allocated for relevant points of knowledge used to address the question. One mark should be given for each relevant, key point of knowledge used to support a factor. If only one factor is presented, a maximum of 3 marks should be given for relevant points of knowledge.

Factors mentioned might include: radical parliamentary reformers, Chartists, party leaders and social changes in education and organisation.

Relevant points of knowledge including:

- The actions of the abolitionists and their motivations: Quakers, William Wilberforce, Olaudah Equiano, Thomas Clarkson, Elizabeth Heyrick, James Stephens, James Ramsay.

- Methods of the abolitionists – judicial challenges, popular campaigning, petitions, a sugar boycott, testimony of ex-slaves, documenting evidence, parliamentary lobbying.

- Using the French war to make opposition to abolition appear unpatriotic in 1807. The abolitionists pioneered the marketing of the abolitionist movement, e.g. through Josiah Wedgewood's pottery.

- Popular pressure outside Parliament supported pressure within Parliament.

- Resistance from the slave traders – the war between Britain and France following the French Revolution 1792–1815 made radical campaigns seem suspicious to many MPs so it took 15 years after the major popular petitions for abolition before the Act abolishing the slave trade was actually passed. In this way it might be said that the actions of the abolitionists delayed the passage of the Bill.

- Events in the Caribbean made passage of the Bill easier – Napoleon re-instituted slavery in the French colonies, making opposition to abolition no longer patriotic.

- Britain captured the French and Dutch Islands that West Indian slave owners had feared would have put them out of business if the British slave trade ended.

- Actions and resistance from slaves themselves, e.g. court cases – James Montgomery and Joseph Knight and slave rebellions in the Caribbean.

- However, it was only the Royal Navy under the instruction of Parliament that could make it happen, so these actions had less impact.

Up to 3 marks should be given for presenting the answer in a structured way, leading to a conclusion which addresses the question as follows:

One mark for the answer being presented in a structured way, with knowledge being organised in support of different factors.

One mark given for a valid judgement or overall conclusion

One mark given for a reason being provided in support of the conclusion.

Part E – The Making of Modern Britain, 1880–1951

Source A is from Seebohm Rowntree's survey of poverty in York published in 1901.

Source A

> We have been accustomed to look upon the poverty in London as exceptional. However, the result of careful investigation shows the proportion of poverty in London is practically equalled in what is a typical provincial town. We are faced with the startling probability that from 25 to 30% of the urban population in the United Kingdom are living in poverty.
>
> That in this land of incredible wealth, in a time of such prosperity never seen before, over a quarter of the population lives in poverty is a fact that may well cause great heart searching.

1. Evaluate the usefulness of **Source A** in explaining changing attitudes towards poverty in Britain.　　**6**

   (You may want to comment on who wrote it, when they wrote it, why they wrote it, what they say or what has been missed out.)

Candidates must evaluate the extent to which a source is useful by commenting on evidence such as the author, type of source, purpose and timing, content and omission.

For a mark to be given, the candidate must identify an aspect of the source and make a comment which shows how this aspect of the source makes the source more or less useful.

Up to the total marks allocation for this question: a maximum of 4 marks can be given for evaluative comments relating to author, type of source, purpose and timing. A maximum of 2 marks may be given for evaluative comments relating to the content of the source. A maximum of 2 marks may be given for points of significant omission.

Candidates can be credited in a number of ways up to a maximum of 6 marks.

Candidates must make a judgement about the usefulness of the source and support this by making evaluative comments on identified aspects of the source.

One mark will be given for each relevant comment made, up to a maximum of 5 marks in total.

Examples of aspects of the source and relevant comments

Author: Seebohm Rowntree.
Comment: Directly involved eyewitness to poverty (a friend of Lloyd George).

Type of source: A factual survey of life in cities.
Comment: Useful, gave decision makers and the better-off in Britain a shocking insight into the life of the poor.

Purpose: To find the reality of poverty in growing towns and cities of industrialised Britain.
Comment: Useful objective of fact-finding, eye-opening for many Victorians.

Timing: 1901.
Comment: Written at a time when there was growing concern about poverty in Britain.

Content: The extent of poverty across the whole country much greater than expected and pause for thought in the light of Britain's unprecedented prosperity.
Comment: Useful – rather than a matter for individual shame, poverty portrayed as a matter of national shame.

Points of significant omission:

- Previously the workhouse system had assumed that poverty was a matter of personal lack of sobriety or care and made support hard to come by

- Also a concern with 'national efficiency' hinted at in the source - a fear that Britain was not competing with Germany and other countries

- Germany already ahead in the use of government welfare to help alleviate poverty

- Quality of army recruits for the Boer War also a concern

2. Explain why the Liberal government introduced reforms to improve the lives of children and the old.   **6**

Candidates must show a causal relationship between events.

Candidates must make a number of points that make the issue plain or clear, for example by showing connections between factors or causal relationships between ideas or events. These should be key reasons and may include theoretical ideas. There is no need for any evaluation or prioritising of these reasons.

Candidates may provide a number of straightforward reasons, a smaller number of developed reasons, or a combination of these.

Up to the total mark allocation for this question: 1 mark should be given for each accurate relevant point. A second mark should be given for any mark that is developed.

Possible reasons may include:

- General motivations for welfare reforms – rise of Labour and Trade Unionism, influence of German welfare reforms, national efficiency and Booth and Rowntree reports on poverty.

- Address issue of undeserved poverty – focus on those unable to help themselves.

- Children, use of education system to identify and address issues of poverty.

- The Boer War created concern about the poor quality of army recruits in terms of fitness and education.

- Free school meals – initially voluntary, compulsory from 1914 to ensure one good meal for poorest children.

- Medical inspections from 1907, provision for treatment from 1912 – but not compulsory for local authorities.

- Notification of Birth Act to quantify and reduce infant mortality – determination of Liberals to ensure Government will take responsibility for the welfare of children.

- Children's Charter reflected idea of children as in need of protection from neglect by parents rather than the business of parents only – Children and Young Persons' Act 1907, punishments for ill treatment of children, forbad sale of tobacco, alcohol or fireworks to children.

- Creation of borstals and young offenders' institutions to give children a chance to escape association with older criminals and possibility of rehabilitation.

- Old people also seen as potentially innocent victims of poverty, but restrictions on Old Age Pensions 1908 designed to incentivise saving for the future – for over 70s only: means-tested and intentionally low, based on Rowntree's 'poverty line' £31 limit, and those out of work for long periods or in prison received nothing, again demonstrating the concern with the innocently poor.

3. To what extent could the creation of the National Health Service be said to be the most successful of the Labour Government's measures between 1945–51? **8**

Candidates must make a judgement about the extent to which different factors contributed to an event or development, or its impact. They are required to provide a balanced account of the influence of different factors and to come to a reasoned conclusion based in the evidence presented.

Up to 5 marks are allocated for relevant points of knowledge used to address the question.

One mark should be given for each relevant, key point of knowledge used to support a factor. If only one factor is presented, a maximum of 3 marks should be given for relevant points of knowledge.

Factors mentioned might include: the establishment of the National Health Service, the Education Act, Housing Acts, National Insurance and National Assistance.

Relevant points of knowledge including:

- The Beveridge Report's identification of 'Five Giants' of disease, ignorance, want, squalor and idleness – a cross-party report in wartime, so agenda not set by Labour alone – Beveridge was a Liberal.

- The obstacles Bevan had to overcome in order to introduce the NHS.

- The things that went well – popularity, a safety net for health that wasn't there before – equitable.

- Problems with the NHS in the early years – expense, the introduction of charges for eye tests, dentistry, prescriptions etc.

- The introduction of Grammar Schools and Secondary Moderns – tackling the giant of ignorance and giving an opportunity for social mobility. Later came under much criticism because of the divisions created by the 11-plus and because the Secondary Moderns did not manage to gain the equal status with Grammar Schools that was intended.

- 1.5 million Council houses built – successful for those who benefited, but only a small dent in the task of replacing houses destroyed in the blitz. Decades later many still lived in the 'temporary' prefabs – prefabricated houses.

- National Insurance Act 1946 extended the coverage of benefits covering sickness and unemployment originally established by the Liberals – not a new development, but did confirm principle of a welfare society. Criticised for thin coverage that left many workers below the poverty line. However, the National Assistance Act 1948 gave a further safety net for those not covered by the National Insurance Act.

- Other relevant points of knowledge.

Up to 3 marks should be given for presenting the answer in a structured way, leading to a conclusion which addresses the question as follows:

One mark for the answer being presented in a structured way, with knowledge being organised in support of different factors.

One mark given for a valid judgement or overall conclusion.

One mark given for a reason being provided in support of the conclusion.

SECTION 3 – EUROPEAN AND WORLD

Part G – Free at last? Civil Rights in the USA, 1918–1968

Sources **A** and **B** are about immigration into America.

Source A

American magazine, *The Atlantic Monthly*, 1907

This horde of immigrants has mainly come since the Irish potato famine of the middle of the last century. The rapid increase year by year has taken the form, not of a steady growth, but of an intermittent flow. First came the people of the British Isles... These were succeeded by the Germans...

More recent still are the Italians, beginning with a modest 20,000 in 1876, rising to over 200,000 arrivals in 1888, and constituting an army of 300,000 in the single year of 1907: and accompanying the Italian has come the great horde of Slavs, Huns, and Jews.

It is the last great wave which has most alarmed us in America.

Source B

After 1890 Italians, Poles, Jews, and Slavs – ethnic groups rarely encountered en masse earlier in American history – arrived in large numbers. Although very many went home again and over 85% of the population remained native born, a significant number settled in America.

Immigrants in New York, Chicago and San Francisco tended to congregate together with their countrymen ... However, during the 1920s – the chain store, the bank branch, the national radio broadcast, and the Hollywood motion picture created, in some cases for the first time, a real common ground that crossed ethnic boundaries in America's cities.

1. Compare the views of **Sources A** and **B** about the nature of immigration into America. (Compare the sources overall and/or in detail.) **4**

Candidates can be credited in a number of ways up to a maximum of 4 marks.

Candidates must make direct comparisons between the two sources either overall or in detail. A simple comparison will indicate what points of detail or overall comparison they agree or disagree about and should be given 1 mark.

A developed comparison in detail or overall viewpoint should be given 2 marks.

Candidates may achieve full marks by making four simple points, two developed points or a combination of these.

Possible points of comparison may include:

Source A	Source B
Overall this source suggests that the most recent wave of immigrants to America has been alarming for those already in America.	Although the latest wave of immigrants at first lived separately, they gradually assimilated into mainstream America.
The most recent immigrants were a 'horde' and an 'army' – reference to invasion.	Many went home again and always vastly outnumbered by those born in America.
Most recent immigrants different from previous waves of immigration.	Agrees that the groups from 1890s on had rarely been encountered before.
Expresses fear and anxiety about recent immigration at the time.	Views the recent immigration in a positive light from a few years later.

2. Describe the activities and influence of the Ku Klux Klan in America after 1918.   **5**

Candidates must make a number of relevant, factual points. These should be key points. The points do not need to be in any particular order. The candidate may provide a number of straightforward points or a smaller number of developed points, or a combination of these.

Up to the total mark allocation for this question: 1 mark should be given for each accurate relevant point of knowledge. A second mark should be given for any point that is developed.

Candidates can be credited in a number of ways up to a maximum of 5 marks. They may take different perspectives on the events and may describe a variety of different aspects of the events.

Possible points of knowledge may include:

- Secret organisation, "Invisible Government".

- Established to defend the values and power of 'WASPS', White Anglo-Saxon Protestants.

- Boosted from 1915 by new waves of non-Protestant immigration and by the popularity of the film "Birth of a Nation" that rekindled interest in the Klan.

- Membership peaked in the 1920s when the KKK spread to Northern States, concerned with immigration, not just the concern of the Southern states defending the Jim Crow Laws.

- Intimidated black people in Southern States who stood up for themselves – burning crosses, large night-time demonstrations, dressed in anonymous hooded costumes.

- Lynching of black people in Southern States who were seen as getting above their station – included beatings as well as hanging.

- Membership included sheriffs, judges and other officials.

- Other valid points.

3. Explain the reasons for the passage of the Civil Rights Act 1964.   **5**

Candidates must show a causal relationship between events.

Candidates must make a number of points that make the issue plain or clear, for example by showing connections between factors or causal relationships between ideas or events. These should be key reasons and may include theoretical ideas. There is no need for any evaluation or prioritising of these reasons.

Candidates may provide a number of straightforward reasons, a smaller number of developed reasons, or a combination of these.

Up to the total mark allocation for this question: 1 mark should be given for each accurate relevant point. A second mark should be given for any mark that is developed.

Possible reasons may include:

- 1960 Civil Rights Act had created the Civil Rights Commission that identified glaring inequalities between black and white Americans.

- Otherwise previous Civil Rights Acts had only a limited impact on segregation.

- Martin Luther King was an international figure due to his campaigns of passive resistance.

- In the Cold War Kennedy had highlighted Civil Rights abuses in Eastern Europe and Cuba – it was more important to address inequalities in America itself.

- The rise of Malcolm X and issues in the ghettoes of American cities threatened to introduce a new militancy and violence into the civil rights debate.

- The assassination of John Kennedy made the passage of the Civil Rights Act more likely against the usual opposition in Congress as it had been a measure associated with JFK – Johnson used this to push it through.

- Johnson was from Texas, which made it easier for him to get southern congressmen to go along with it.

- By January 1964 public opinion was overwhelmingly in favour of passing the Civil Rights Act.

- Other valid relevant points.

Source C is about the Black Panther Party.

Source C

The Panthers were strongly influenced by Stokley Carmichael, Chairman of the SNCC who had called on "... black people in this country to unite, to recognize their heritage, to build a sense of community. It is a call for black people to define their own goals, to lead their own organizations." .... The Black Panthers focused more upon grass roots action, such as their Free Breakfast for Children program and their campaigns against police brutality. Their military-style uniforms and militant language seemed intimidating to many mainstream Americans and J Edgar Hoover, Director of the FBI called them "the greatest threat to the internal security of the country".

4. How fully does **Source C** explain the impact of militant campaigns for civil rights in America? (Use **Source C** and recall.) **6**

Candidates must make an overall judgement about the extent to which the source provides a full description/explanation of a given event or development.

One mark will be given for each valid point interpreted from the source or each valid point of significant omission provided.

The candidate can achieve up to 3 marks for their interpretation of the parts of the source they consider relevant in terms of the proposed question, where there is also at least one point of significant omission identified to imply a judgement has been made about the limitations of the source.

For full marks to be given each point needs to be discretely mentioned in terms of the question.

Possible points that may be mentioned from the source include:

- The Black Panthers were inspired by the idea that black people should set their own goals and build a sense of community rather than aspiring to be a part of mainstream American society.

- Organised practical grassroots action to improve life in black communities in American cities, such as breakfast clubs to encourage children to stay in school and campaigns against police brutality.

- The military uniforms and appearance of the Black Panthers was intimidating to many Americans.

- The FBI regarded militant black activism as threatening to America as a whole.

Possible points of omission include:

- Militant campaigners had become impatient with Martin Luther King's campaign, which depended on support from white America.

- Dealing with the economic issues in the ghettoes of northern cities was more complicated than the more clear-cut discrimination of segregation in the south.

- Malcolm X was a member of the Nation of Islam, which believed in a radical separation between black and white America.

- Carmichael encouraged Black communities to put pressure on elected representatives.

By the 1970s the Black Power movement had lost influence having failed to make inroads into mainstream black society.

Part I – World War II, 1939–1945

1. Explain the reasons for the success of the tactic of Blitzkreig in the early months of World War Two. **5**

Candidates must show a causal relationship between events.

Candidates must make a number of points that make the issue plain or clear, for example by showing connections between factors or causal relationships between ideas or events. These should be key reasons and may include theoretical ideas. There is no need for any evaluation or prioritising of these reasons.

Candidates may provide a number of straightforward reasons, a smaller number of developed reasons, or a combination of these.

Up to the total mark allocation for this question: 1 mark should be given for each accurate relevant point. A second mark should be given for any mark that is developed.

Possible reasons may include:

- Surprise – Blitzkreig required an element of surprise.

- For example, in the invasion of France May 1940 the German Panzers passed through the supposedly impenetrable Belgian Ardennes Forest, so met relatively little resistance from French troops defending the border with Germany.

- Speed – Blitzkreig was supposed to break through a weak spot in the enemy lines using mechanised vehicles – tanks, trucks, motorbikes and aircraft that could move quickly deep behind enemy lines before the defenders could react.

- Co-ordination – different types of forces would work closely together using radio communication so that paratroops, bombing of enemy communications, towns and Stuka bombers and fighters strafing refugees would cause chaos and confusion.

- This tactic had originally been used by the British in the last months of World War One, but had been abandoned and forgotten.

- The French put all of their efforts into the development of the static defences of the Maginot Line so had not given great consideration to these kinds of tactics.

- Other relevant and accurate points.

Sources A and **B** are about the Japanese attack on Pearl Harbour in November 1941.

Source A

> While occupying French Indochina in July 1941, Japan knew that a full-scale invasion of South-east Asia would prompt war with America. It needed a mechanism to buy itself sufficient time and space to conquer successfully crucial targets like the Philippines, Burma and Malaya. The attack on Pearl Harbor was that mechanism; merely a means to an end. By destroying its Pacific Fleet, Japan expected to remove America from the Pacific equation for long enough to allow it to secure the resources it needed so desperately and hoped to crush American morale sufficiently to prompt Roosevelt to sue for peace.

Source B

> The Japanese were tired of negotiations with the United States. They wanted to continue their expansion within Asia but the United States had placed an extremely restrictive embargo on Japan in the hopes of curbing Japan's aggression. Negotiations to solve their differences hadn't been going well.
>
> Rather than giving in to U.S. demands, the Japanese decided to launch a surprise attack against the United States in an attempt to destroy the United States' naval power even before an official announcement of war was given.

2. Compare the views of **Sources A** and **B** about the reasons for the Japanese attack on Pearl Harbour (Compare the sources overall and/ or in detail).   **4**

Candidates can be credited in a number of ways up to a maximum of 4 marks.

Candidates must make direct comparisons between the two sources either overall or in detail. A simple comparison will indicate what points of detail or overall comparison they agree or disagree about and should be given one mark. A developed comparison in detail or overall viewpoint should be given 2 marks.

Candidates may achieve full marks by making four simple points, two developed points or a combination of these.

Possible points of comparison may include:

Source A	*Source B*
Overall, the Japanese were taking a planned calculated risk to make time for the expansion of the Japanese empire.	Overall the Japanese reacted violently to growing tensions rather than planning ahead.
Pearl Harbour attack was a means to an end not a way of winning the war.	To strike first to gain advantage in a war that seemed inevitable.
Planned invasion of South East Asia would provoke a war with America.	Japan tired of the US embargo and reacting to the negotiations going badly.
Pearl Harbour intended to inflict enough damage that Roosevelt would sue for peace.	The Japanese hoped to destroy the American fleet once and for all.

Source C is about Nazi-occupied Europe.

Source C

The harshness of Nazi occupation varied according to the status of the occupied land. In *Mein Kampf*, Hitler had made plain his racial theories: he hated the Jews and Slavs and believed in the 'supremacy' of the Aryan race. It was therefore those unfortunate enough to live to the East of Germany who experienced the greatest cruelty. In the west the Germans were content to take control, using local politicians if possible. In Norway for example, Major Quisling took charge; and in the area of France not occupied by the Germans (Vichy France) the French First World War hero, Marshal Petain, headed the government. Even in the west, however, Nazi rule was backed up by terror tactics enforced by the hated Gestapo and black-uniformed SS.

3. How fully does **Source C** explain the experience of those living under German occupation in World War Two? (Use **Source C** and recall.)   **6**

Candidates must make an overall judgement about the extent to which the source provides a full description/explanation of a given event or development.

One mark will be given for each valid point interpreted from the source or each valid point of significant omission provided. The candidate can achieve up to 3 marks for their interpretation of the parts of the source they consider relevant in terms of the proposed question, where there is also at least one point of significant omission identified to imply a judgement has been made about the limitations of the source.

For full marks to be given each point needs to be discretely mentioned in terms of the question.

Possible points that may be mentioned from the source include:

*   Hitler hated Jews and Slavs, which had an impact on how people were treated in different parts of Nazi-occupied Europe.

*   Those in occupied Eastern Europe experienced the harshest treatment under the Nazis.

*   In western occupied countries the Germans ruled through local leaders who were willing to collaborate, such as Quisling and Petain.

*   In the western occupied countries the occupied peoples were still subject to the terroristic regime of the Gestapo and the SS.

Possible points of omission include:

*   The Nazis took raw materials from Eastern occupied countries and citizens were on minimum rations.

*   Some civilians transported to Germany to undertake forced labour.

*   Resistance movements developed in occupied countries – carried out acts of sabotage to disrupt the German war effort.

- The Nazis carried out reprisals, e.g. destruction of Lidice in Czechoslovakia in revenge for the assassination of Heydrich.

- In Denmark a Reichsminister ruled directly.

- Any other substantial and relevant point of recall.

4. Describe the role of the Russian Army in bringing about the defeat of Germany. **5**

Candidates must make a number of relevant, factual points. These should be key points. The points do not need to be in any particular order. The candidate may provide a number of straightforward points or a smaller number of developed points, or a combination of these.

Up to the total mark allocation for this question: 1 mark should be given for each accurate relevant point of knowledge. A second mark should be given for any point that is developed.

Candidates can be credited in a number of ways up to a maximum of 5 marks. They may take different perspectives on the events and may describe a variety of different aspects of the events.

Possible points of knowledge may include:

- The Red Army had been weakened by purges and performed poorly at the start of the war.

- In the first few weeks of Operation Barbarossa tens of thousands of Russian soldiers were captured.

- The scorched earth policy and the formation of guerrilla units helped to undermine the German war effort.

- Operation Uranus encircled the German Sixth Army.

- Stalingrad and the Battle of Kursk, 1943, were turning points in the war in the East.

- Soviet victories were an example to the West that the Nazi war machine could be beaten.

- Twelve and a half million soldiers fought in the Red Army at its peak.

- Lend lease from allies gave the Soviet Union the resources to compete.

- Huge effort in production of military equipment allowed the Soviet Army to compete.

- The opening up of a second front with D-Day alongside the advance of the Red Army towards Berlin meant that Germany was fighting on two fronts.

SECTION 1 – SCOTTISH

Part A – The Wars of Independence, 1286–1328

1. Describe the problems caused for Scotland by the death of Alexander III.   **5**

Candidates must make a number of relevant, factual points. These should be key points. The points do not need to be in any particular order. The candidate may provide a number of straightforward points or a smaller number of developed points, or a combination of these.

Up to the total mark allocation for this question: 1 mark should be given for each accurate relevant point of knowledge. A second mark should be given for any point that is developed.

Candidates can be credited in a number of ways up to a maximum of 5 marks. They may take different perspectives on the events and may describe a variety of different aspects of the events.

Possible points of knowledge may include:

- No immediate strong heir to the throne.

- Maid of Norway, a young child, lived in Norway.

- Competing claims of powerful nobles threaten civil war if power vacuum persists.

- No provision for Margaret's minority because of unexpected death.

- Community of the Realm under six guardians.

- Looking for greater security through Treaty of Birgham with Edward I – would create problems of its own later.

- Edward only alternative source of authority.

- Possibility of an alternative heir briefly from Alexander's second marriage to Yolande.

- Unexpected double blow with the death of Margaret in Orkney.

2. Explain the reasons for the Franco-Scottish treaty of October 1295.   **5**

Candidates must make a number of points that make the issue plain or clear, for example by showing connections between factors or causal relationships between ideas or events. These should be key reasons and may include theoretical ideas. There is no need for any evaluation or prioritising of these reasons.

Candidates may provide a number of straightforward reasons, a smaller number of developed reasons, or a combination of these.

Up to the total mark allocation for this question: 1 mark should be given for each accurate relevant point. A second mark should be given for any mark that is developed.

Possible reasons may include:

- Edward's demand that his overlordship be recognised.

- King John Balliol did homage to Edward at Newcastle.

- Continuing role of the Kingdom of the Realm / remaining guardians.

- Pressure on John to stand up for his rights as King of Scots.

- Edward's confiscation of castles of Edinburgh, Roxburgh and Stirling.

- Edwards wars with France and Wales.

- Edward's demand for military support from John and his Earls and Barons.

- France treated Scots as equals rather than as a client state.

- Philip IV of France recognised the status of the Community of the Realm.

- John forced to renounce his fealty to Edward.

- Sealed the 'Auld Alliance'.

Source A is about the Scottish uprising against Edward in 1297.

Source A

> Although the origins of the revolt of 1297 have been known to historians for a long time, the idea persists that it was a spontaneous rebellion of landless peasants led by Wallace. It is true that many of the Scottish nobility were in English prisons or had been killed in previous battles. The first outbreaks happened in the north rather than in Wallace's territory. Together Murray, son of a baron and leader of the northern rising, and Wallace were acknowledged as 'commanders of the army of the community of the realm'. Neither a general nor a guerrilla by instinct, Wallace nonetheless deserves to be remembered as an unflinching patriot and a charismatic warlord. That was why the community entrusted him with sole Guardianship of the realm in the Spring of 1298.

3. How fully does **Source A** explain the role played by William Wallace in the Wars of Independence? (Use **Source A** and recall.)   **5**

Candidates must make an overall judgement about the extent to which the source provides a full description/explanation of a given event or development.

One mark will be given for each valid point interpreted from the source or each valid point of significant omission provided. The candidate can achieve up to 3 marks for their interpretation of the parts of the source they consider relevant in terms of the proposed question, where there is also at least one point of significant omission identified to imply a judgement has been made about the limitations of the source.

For full marks to be given each point needs to be discretely mentioned in terms of the question.

Possible points that may be mentioned from the source include:

- Initially the uprising was not centred on the area where Wallace operated.

- Murray and Wallace emerged as joint leaders.

- Wallace was not a natural tactician.

- His bravery and charisma was acknowledged by the community of the realm when he was made sole Guardian.

Possible points of omission include:

- Wallace may have played some part along with Murray in devising the tactics that were so successful at the Battle of Stirling Bridge.

- Initially there were several leaders – the revolt was first led by former guardians, Robert Wishart, the Bishop of Glasgow and James Stewart, Wallace's lord.

- Stirling Bridge was a turning point – Wallace went on the attack in harrying the north.

- As Guardian he looked to have Scotland's case as an independent kingdom recognised abroad.

- Provided an example for Bruce's later campaigns.

- Defeat at Falkirk – tactically outmanoeuvred by Edward, 1298.

- Capture, trial and execution at Westminster.

Source B is from the *Lanercrost Chronicle*, a history of the Wars of Independence written shortly afterwards by monks living in a priory in the north of England. It describes the Battle of Bannockburn.

Source B

> When both armies engaged each other and the great horses of the English charged the pikes of the Scots like into a dense forest, there arose a great and terrible crash of spears broken and of the horses wounded to death. Now the English in the rear could not reach the Scots because the leading division was in the way, nor could they do anything to help themselves, so there was nothing for it but to take flight. This account I heard from a trustworthy person who was present as an eyewitness.

4. Evaluate the usefulness of **Source B** in explaining the reasons for Bruce's victory at Bannockburn.   **5**

   (You may want to comment on who wrote it, when they wrote it, why they wrote it, what they say or what has been missed out.)

Candidates must evaluate the extent to which a source is useful by commenting on evidence such as the author, type of source, purpose and timing, content and omission.

For a mark to be given, the candidate must identify an aspect of the source and make a comment which shows how this aspect of the source makes the source more or less useful.

Up to the total marks allocation for this question: a maximum of 4 marks can be given for evaluative comments relating to author, type of source, purpose and timing. A maximum of 2 marks may be given for evaluative comments relating to the content of the source. A maximum of 2 marks may be given for points of significant omission.

Candidates can be credited in a number of ways up to a maximum of 5 marks.

Candidates must make a judgement about the usefulness of the source and support this by making evaluative comments on identified aspects of the source.

One mark will be given for each relevant comment made, up to a maximum of 5 marks in total.

Examples of aspects of the source and relevant comments

Author: The *Lanercrost Chronicle*.
Comment: Useful because written by monks – the best–educated people from the late 13th and early 14th centuries.

Type of source: A chronicle.
Comment: Attempt to write an accurate record of events, so quite useful and does not appear to be biased.

Purpose: An attempt to describe events.
Comment: Objective purpose.

Timing: An almost contemporaneous source.
Comment: Written shortly afterwards so may have had reasonably close access to first hand/ knowledgeable sources, which it mentions explicitly.

Content: Emphasises the role of the Scots pike men and lack of room for manoeuvre by knights in explaining the English defeat.
Comment: These were key reasons for the Scots defeating the English at Bannockburn, but does not show the whole picture.

Points of significant omission:

- The inability of the English to manoeuvre explained by the course of the river and marshy land.

- Defection of Seton with his intelligence about English deployment overnight after the first day of the battle.

- Offensive use of schiltroms hinted at but not clear in the account.

- English unable to use their advantage in archery due to the melée.

Part C – The Treaty of Union, 1689–1715

1. Describe the problems caused for Scotland by the failure of the Darien Scheme.   **5**

Candidates must make a number of relevant, factual points. These should be key points. The points do not need to be in any particular order. The candidate may provide a number of straightforward points or a smaller number of developed points, or a combination of these.

Up to the total mark allocation for this question: 1 mark should be given for each accurate relevant point of knowledge. A second mark should be given for any point that is developed.

Candidates can be credited in a number of ways up to a maximum of 5 marks. They may take different perspectives on the events and may describe a variety of different aspects of the events.

Possible points of knowledge include:

- East India Company and Spanish threats caused withdrawal of foreign investment.

- Around £400 000, one-fifth of the wealth of Scotland was invested in the scheme.

- Trading decline and dependence on English trade prior to the Darien Adventure.

- Blamed English for failure – king refused to back another attempt for fear of war with Spain.

- Those associated with the scheme shunned.

- Disastrous loss of the *Speedy Return* and the *Continent,* trying to make good the loss of Darien.

- Capture of the *Annandale* by the East India Company for 'illegally' attempting trade with the Spice Islands.

- Hanging of the innocent crew of the *Worcester* reflection of frustration of Scottish public.

- Link to Union – Commissioners particularly indebted.

- Scotland unable to go on alone.

- Article 14 of the Treaty of Union included the 'Equivalent' replacing losses of Darien Scheme and offset future indemnities against the English National Debt.

- Lingering resentment played a part in Jacobite rebellions.

Source A discusses the reasons for the introduction of the Treaty of Union.

Source A

> Those who hold the idea that Union was bound to happen have to take into account the particular circumstances that brought it about. It needed a freak coincidence of short-term factors that actually made the passage of a union bill possible. In 1702 there was virtually no support in the English parliament for a union; by 1704 circumstances pointed to a treaty to secure the succession being the most likely outcome. In the autumn of 1708 the position of the Whigs, architects of the Union's passage through Parliament were in trouble and losing support because of the cost of the War of the Spanish Succession and they would not have risked anything as risky as the Act of Union. The bill passed in the eye of a storm that made the unlikely a certainty.

2. How fully does **Source A** explain the reasons for the successful passage of the Treaty of Union? **5**

Candidates must make an overall judgement about the extent to which the source provides a full description/explanation of a given event or development.

One mark will be given for each valid point interpreted from the source or each valid point of significant omission provided.

The candidate can achieve up to 3 marks for their interpretation of the parts of the source they consider relevant in terms of the proposed question, where there is also at least one point of significant omission identified to imply a judgement has been made about the limitations of the source.

For full marks to be given each point needs to be discretely mentioned in terms of the question.

Possible points that may be mentioned from the source include:

- There was virtually no support for the Union in 1702.

- By 1704 the Union had become very likely.

- If the Whigs had tried to pass it later it would not have succeeded because of the War of the Spanish Succession.

- Only brief 'freak factors' made its passage possible.

Possible points of omission include:

- There were many long-term reasons for pushing for Union both in England and Scotland.

- The personal union of the crowns made political union more likely.

- For the English wars and tension with France made the continuing of the Auld Alliance undesirable.

- The English Parliament had twice deposed the Scots King – also their own – without consulting the Scots.

- This was the first time that there was sufficient support in both England and Scotland for Union, but for different reasons – finance/Protestant succession.

- Followed a period of heightened tensions between England and Scotland.

3. Explain the reasons for unrest in Edinburgh and elsewhere during the passage of the Treaty of Union. **5**

Candidates must make a number of points that make the issue plain or clear, for example by showing connections between factors or causal relationships between ideas or events. These should be key reasons and may include theoretical ideas. There is no need for any evaluation or prioritising of these reasons.

Candidates may provide a number of straightforward reasons, a smaller number of developed reasons, or a combination of these.

Up to the total mark allocation for this question: 1 mark should be given for each accurate relevant point. A second mark should be given for any mark that is developed.

Possible reasons may include:

- Little unrest in 1706, prior to passage of the Bill itself.

- Increasing acceptance from governing classes and professionals – realisation of likelihood it would pass.

- Publication of Articles and focus of protests on Parliament building.

- Concerns about taxation.

- Concerns of and resistance of the Kirk – loss of the Church's independence.

- November 1706 quietened in Edinburgh through use of troops, led to protests, moved more in country, but less focused.

- Dismissal of petitions.

Source B is from a letter written by the Earl of Mar to the Earl of Oxford in 1711 discussing his feelings following the Treaty of Union.

Source B

> I am not yet weary of the Union, but still think that if used well [it is] for the good of the whole island and also that it is the only thing which can preserve Scotland, and England too, from Blood and confusion, so I do not at all repent the part I had in it. But should that hardship of the Peeradge (taxation) be put upon us against all sense, reason and fair dealing and if our trade is not more encouraged than it has been so far, or seems likely at the moment, how is it possible that flesh and blood can bear it and what Scots man will not be weary of the union and do all he can to get rid of it?

4. Evaluate the usefulness of **Source B** in explaining the impact of the Treaty of Union in Scotland.   5

   (You may want to comment on who wrote it, when they wrote it, why they wrote it, what they say or what has been missed out.)

Candidates must evaluate the extent to which a source is useful by commenting on evidence such as the author, type of source, purpose and timing, content and omission.

For a mark to be given, the candidate must identify an aspect of the source and make a comment which shows how this aspect of the source makes the source more or less useful.

Up to the total marks allocation for this question: a maximum of 4 marks can be given for evaluative comments relating to author, type of source, purpose and timing. A maximum of 2 marks may be given for evaluative comments relating to the content of the source. A maximum of 2 marks may be given for points of significant omission.

Candidates can be credited in a number of ways up to a maximum of 5 marks.

Candidates must make a judgement about the usefulness of the source and support this by making evaluative comments on identified aspects of the source.

One mark will be given for each relevant comment made, up to a maximum of 5 marks in total.

Examples of aspects of the source and relevant comments

Author: Earl of Mar Commissioner and supporter of the Union in 1707, but would later lead Jacobite Rebellion.
Comment: It shows that some people changed their mind about the Union

Type of source: A private letter.
Comment: Likely to be honest about his feelings about the Union, but not necessarily objective.

Purpose: Explaining his feelings about the Union.
Comment: Useful focus on the economic and political effects from his viewpoint.

Timing: Four years after the Union.
Comment: Useful as he is still in transition and can see potential benefits, but awareness of drawbacks becoming apparent.

Content:

- He still believes that on balance the Union has been beneficial in preserving the peace and security of Scotland as well as England.

- But growing discontent at the lack of economic benefits to Scotland and burden of unfair taxation on Scotland.

Comment: Useful as it suggests that the economic benefits or penalties to Scotland played an important part in disquiet with Union in the succeeding years.

Points of significant omission:

- It took 30 years for Scots to benefit economically from Union.

- Merchant navy benefited, however and Scots became an important part of the East India Company.

- Scottish religious opinion split – Presbyterians reassured initially by the Act of Security, Episcopalians opposed.

- Mar would go on to lead a rebellion of Jacobites, but opposed by Scots as well as English.

SECTION 2 – BRITISH

Part C – War of the Three Kingdoms, 1603–1651

1. Explain the reasons for conflict between the Crown and Parliament in the reign of James I.   **6**

Candidates must show a causal relationship between events.

Candidates must make a number of points that make the issue plain or clear, for example by showing connections between factors or causal relationships between ideas or events. These should be key reasons and may include theoretical ideas. There is no need for any evaluation or prioritising of these reasons.

Candidates may provide a number of straightforward reasons, a smaller number of developed reasons, or a combination of these.

Up to the total mark allocation for this question: 1 mark should be given for each accurate relevant point. A second mark should be given for any mark that is developed.

Possible reasons may include:

- Finance
    - James had not been prosperous as King in Scotland and expected to have a much more lavish lifestyle as king of a richer kingdom.
    - While Queen Elizabeth had been unmarried, James' family were far more expensive to finance – £25 000 per annum set aside for Prince Henry.
    - James wanted clothing for a king to match the late queen's wardrobe – spending on clothing rose from £10 000 to £36 000 between 1603 and 1610.
    - Members of the Scottish court came to London – as poorer nobles, James subsidised their lifestyles with pensions and gifts to the tune of £90 000. Some English nobles resented this.
    - James paid off the debts of his favourites, e.g. Carr.
    - Robert Cecil tried to reduce the debts with new methods of finance, e.g. impositions – Parliament greatly resented this.
    - The only attempt to get to the heart of Royal finances was the Great Contract of 1610, which fell short of a solution because of the amount Parliament was prepared to grant in exchange for ending impositions.
    - The Addled Parliament, 1614, short-lived partly because of disputes over finance.

- The Divine Right of Kings
    - James believed that monarchs were ordained by God to rule without restriction and resented Parliament's questioning of his spending or policy.

- Favourites
    - James' promotion and entitlement of favourites like Robert Carr and Villiers, often from humble backgrounds, offended many members of parliament, as did James's taking advice from these and other advisors.

- Foreign policy
  - The Thirty Years' War was perceived by many nobles to be a war of religion between Protestants and Roman Catholics. James' favourite, Buckingham, tried to promote good relations with Spain, the major Catholic power.

2. To what extent did Charles I's own actions create the crisis that led to war in 1642?   **6**

Candidates must make a judgement about the extent to which different factors contributed to an event or development, or its impact. They are required to provide a balanced account of the influence of different factors and to come to a reasoned conclusion based in the evidence presented.

Up to 5 marks are allocated for relevant points of knowledge used to address the question.

One mark should be given for each relevant, key point of knowledge used to support a factor. If only one factor is presented, a maximum of 3 marks should be given for relevant points of knowledge.

Factors mentioned might include inherited problems, Charles' actions in finance, religion and treatment of MPs, Parliament's actions:

- Charles inherited some of the unresolved financial problems of his father – rather than an established and regular source of adequate income for the Crown, Charles collected innovative forms of taxation that Parliament resented – The Petition of Right 1628 came early in Charles' reign and reflected on issues between James and Parliament not just Charles. Ship Money, 1834, which had a disastrous impact on relations with Parliament, was in this tradition.

- However, Charles made some of these things worse, for example applying Ship Money to inland towns and starting his reign working through his father's widely-hated favourite, Buckingham, instead of making a fresh start.

- Charles also made things worse by trying to take on Parliament on too many fronts at once, e.g. while trying to persuade Parliament to grant finance for wars with France and Spain he tried to reintroduce the 39 articles, which were regarded as too Catholic by members of Parliament. In return the Three Resolutions made it clear that MPs linked the Petition of Right to religion as well as to finance.

- Charles' belief in the Divine Right of Kings made him high-handed in his treatment of MPs, arresting nine in 1629 and, fatefully, five in January 1642. This was the final straw that led to the formation of armies for war.

- Charles managed to go to war with a parliament that was desperate to avoid it.

- Charles was unrealistic in his treatment of religion, particularly in Scotland – his support for Archbishop Laud's policies were his responsibility and led directly to the crisis that led to war with Parliament as he tried to get funding for a war with the Covenanters.

- Parliament should bear some responsibility, particularly for not co-operating in the creation of a better system of taxation to help the Crown finances.

- Parliament also bears responsibility for the crisis that emerged in Ireland, as the removal of Wentworth as Lord Deputy in Ireland (beheaded in May 1641), who had upset Protestant interests there, was a mistake. The rebellion in Ireland that followed brought the crisis to a head as it had the effect of raising fears of a Catholic invasion and of giving Charles the funds and authority to raise his own army.

Up to 3 marks should be given for presenting the answer in a structured way, leading to a conclusion which addresses the question as follows:

One mark for the answer being presented in a structured way, with knowledge being organised in support of different factors.

One mark given for a valid judgement or overall conclusion.

One mark given for a reason being provided in support of the conclusion.

Source A Is from a book of essays by John Selden, who fought in the Civil War, written in 1689.

Source A

> If men would say they took arms for anything but religion, they might have been put off by reasoning; but when they fight for that reason they never can be.
>
> At the heart of pretending that religion is the cause of all wars is because it is the one thing to be found that all men might have an interest in. In this the poor groom might have as much interest as the lord. If they were to fight for land one owns a thousand acres and the other just one; the latter would not risk as much as the one who has a thousand. But religion means as much to both. Had all men the same amount of land by some agrarian law, then all men would say they fought for land.

3. Evaluate the usefulness of **Source A** as evidence of the reasons soldiers used to choose sides in the civil war. **6**

   (You may want to comment on who wrote it, when they wrote it, why they wrote it, what they say or what has been missed out.)

Candidates must evaluate the extent to which a source is useful by commenting on evidence such as the author, type of source, purpose and timing, content and omission.

For a mark to be given, the candidate must identify an aspect of the source and make a comment which shows how this aspect of the source makes the source more or less useful.

Up to the total marks allocation for this question: a maximum of 4 marks can be given for evaluative comments relating to author, type of source, purpose and timing. A maximum of 2 marks may be given for evaluative comments relating to the content of the source. A maximum of 2 marks may be given for points of significant omission.

Candidates can be credited in a number of ways up to a maximum of 5 marks.

Candidates must make a judgement about the usefulness of the source and support this by making evaluative comments on identified aspects of the source.

One mark will be given for each relevant comment made, up to a maximum of 5 marks in total.

Examples of aspects of the source and relevant comments

Author: John Selden.
Comment: He lived through the civil war and could speak from experience about why people chose sides, so this is useful.

Type of source: A published book.
Comment: Selden has had time to reflect on events and is giving his honest view of people's motivations, so this is useful.

Purpose: A general essay on why people fight.
Comment: Although a general essay, Selden's experience is based on the War of the Three Kingdoms, so it is relevant and useful.

Timing: 1689.
Comment: This is a long time after the events of Selden's youth – on the one hand this makes his judgement cooler, which is useful, but he may also have misremembered or had his views coloured by things that happened since the 1640s.

Content: Religion was the most important motivation because it is the one thing that moved everyone to fight with the same passion. Land and wealth was only important to the rich.
Comment: This is useful, because although Cavaliers were often portrayed as the rich and Roundheads as the poor side in the conflict, in fact both rich and poor fought on both sides. Religion was also a key factor for those who fought in Scotland and Ireland at the start of the war.

Points of significant omission:

- Although religion was important at the start in bringing things to a head, later the Scots allied themselves with the king against Parliament.

- At the start of the war Parliament sided with the Scottish Covenanters who were at war with Charles, which appeared unpatriotic, so some in England became Royalists out of patriotism.

- Others pointed to Charles' apparent attempt to use 'foreign' troops and so saw supporting Parliament as a patriotic defender of Englishness. For this reason, on the other hand many Cornish and Welsh chose to support the King against the 'English' parliamentarians.

- The War was also fundamentally about the Divine Right of Kings and the rights of Parliament and many chose sides depending on where they stood on this issue.

- The personality of Charles played a part in choice of side also – he had a gift for alienating those who wanted to work with him.

- As the Civil War went on concerns about class did become important as the emergence of the Levellers and Diggers made clear.

- There were many who fought without passion – called to fight by landlords, press-ganged or conscripted, while foreign mercenaries cared little for the issues at stake.

Part D – Changing Britain, 1760–1900

Source A is from a Factory Inspector's report written in 1836.

Source A

> They stated to me that they commenced work on Friday morning and … they did not cease working until four o'clock on Saturday evening, having been two days and a night thus engaged. I asked every boy the same questions and from each received the same answers. I then went into the house to look at the time book and, in the presence of the masters, referred to the cruelty of the case and stated that I should certainly punish it with all the severity in my power. Mr Rayner, the certificated surgeon of Bastile was with me at the time.

1. Evaluate the usefulness of **Source A** as evidence of the impact of technology and legislation on textile factories in Britain. **6**

   (You may want to comment on who wrote it, when they wrote it, why they wrote it, what they say or what has been missed out.)

Candidates must evaluate the extent to which a source is useful by commenting on evidence such as the author, type of source, purpose and timing, content and omission.

For a mark to be given, the candidate must identify an aspect of the source and make a comment which shows how this aspect of the source makes the source more or less useful.

Up to the total marks allocation for this question: a maximum of 4 marks can be given for evaluative comments relating to author, type of source, purpose and timing. A maximum of 2 marks may be given for evaluative comments relating to the content of the source. A maximum of 2 marks may be given for points of significant omission.

Candidates can be credited in a number of ways up to a maximum of 5 marks.

Candidates must make a judgement about the usefulness of the source and support this by making evaluative comments on identified aspects of the source.

One mark will be given for each relevant comment made, up to a maximum of 5 marks in total.

Examples of aspects of the source and relevant comments

Author: 19th-century factory inspector.
Comment: Useful – knowledgeable and unbiased about the issue.

Type of source: Factory inspection report.
Comment: Useful – unbiased investigation into factory conditions.

Purpose: To investigate the treatment of workers in one particular factory.
Comment: Helpful in outlining both how technology affected conditions, the impact of previous legislation and why later legislation was introduced.

Timing: 1836.
Comment: Very useful – shortly after the passing of the most effective of the early factory acts 1833.

Content: The inspector found boys in the factory required to work two days and a night without a rest.
Comment: Useful – shows that factory machinery permitted work through the night – before legislation people had to work to the pace of the machines, but factory legislation began to bring such practices to book.

Points of significant omission:

- Technological innovation in textiles started in the 18th Century with the power loom and Richard Arkwright's factory, amongst others.

- The development of factories accelerated with the use of steam.

- When families worked together in textile factories they were taking practices from agricultural working into factories.

- Legislation to deal with concerns about conditions in factories began in 1819. After 1833 concern moved from children to encompass all textile factory workers.

2. Explain the reasons for radical unrest in the first half of the 19th century in Britain.　　**6**

Candidates must show a causal relationship between events.

Candidates must make a number of points that make the issue plain or clear, for example by showing connections between factors or causal relationships between ideas or events. These should be key reasons and may include theoretical ideas. There is no need for any evaluation or prioritising of these reasons.

Candidates may provide a number of straightforward reasons, a smaller number of developed reasons, or a combination of these.

Up to the total mark allocation for this question: 1 mark should be given for each accurate relevant point. A second mark should be given for any mark that is developed.

Possible reasons may include:

- The influence of the French Revolution – radical speakers such as Henry Hunt and Major Cartwright's Hampden Clubs spread radical ideas.

- Economic downturn following Napoleonic Wars – anger turned on protection of landowners through the Corn Laws with its perceived impact on the price of bread.

- Anger at the Liverpool Government – Six Acts and the Peterloo massacre.

- Cato Street conspiracy, 1820, clearly inspired by French Revolution – plot to murder the cabinet.

- Industrial change and disruption, e.g. Luddite machine breakers.

- Urbanisation and suffering resulting from new conditions in factories etc.

- Scotland – radical war of 1820 – threatened General Strike through the influence of 'corresponding societies'.

- Jeremy Bentham and the spread of utilitarian ideas in 1820s refocused attention on rational arguments for radical reform – Political Unions and discontent spilling onto the streets 1830–32.

- Following Great Reform Act, 1832, those who did not benefit focused efforts into Chartism – peaceful and violent wings, but also Anti-Corn Law League reflected a different explanation of working class grievances.

- Changes in the methods of production led to the decline of the handloom weavers, machine breaking etc.

3. To what extent were changes to industry in Britain the result of developments in transport?   **8**

Candidates must make a judgement about the extent to which different factors contributed to an event or development, or its impact. They are required to provide a balanced account of the influence of different factors and to come to a reasoned conclusion based in the evidence presented.

Up to 5 marks are allocated for relevant points of knowledge used to address the question.

One mark should be given for each relevant, key point of knowledge used to support a factor. If only one factor is presented, a maximum of 3 marks should be given for relevant points of knowledge.

Factors mentioned might include: canals, railways, political stability, raw materials, machinery and the factory system.

Relevant points of knowledge including:

- Canals were much better than roads for transporting heavy goods, such as coal, and fragile goods, such as pottery, to town – faster than roads.

- 1790s canals were highly profitable and 'canal mania' took off – 4500 miles of canals by 1840s – this allowed more coal and other goods to be transported more quickly, more cheaply and at greater profit, accelerating the development of factories and towns.

- Canals began to decline from the middle of 19th Century as roads improved and railways took over. Canals had disadvantages – they were too slow to carry perishable food stuffs and different engineers built canals in different sizes, restricting their spread. Canals were also more vulnerable to bad weather – freezing and drought.

- Railways – more reliable, faster and more flexible than canals.

- Railways enabled the connection of raw materials to factory production, so that production could happen in places more convenient to trade, while also linking trade routes.

- By 1850s tens of thousands of miles of track being built, leading to the rapid growth of cities, no longer tied to waterways for communications.

- Raw materials – growing population's fuel needs could not be met by wood alone – the abundance of coal in Britain key to the rapid development of factories and underpinned the use of steam power on a great scale.

- Coal provides three times more energy than wood.

- Iron ore also abundant.

- Politics – the stability of the political system following the 'Glorious Revolution' of 1688 – no violent revolution and with little change in the government of the country allowed industry to develop.

- As did the 'laissez-faire' approach of Government, which allowed the free flow of new scientific ideas.

- The development of the empire also created new markets for industrial production.

- Transport by sail, then steam ships, crucial also.

Up to 3 marks should be given for presenting the answer in a structured way, leading to a conclusion which addresses the question as follows:

One mark for the answer being presented in a structured way, with knowledge being organised in support of different factors.

One mark given for a valid judgement or overall conclusion.

One mark given for a reason being provided in support of the conclusion.

SECTION 3 – EUROPEAN AND WORLD

Part F: Mussolini and Fascist Italy, 1919–1939

1. Explain the reasons for the weakness of the Italian state in 1919.   **5**

Candidates must make a number of points that make the issue plain or clear, for example by showing connections between factors or causal relationships between ideas or events. These should be key reasons and may include theoretical ideas. There is no need for any evaluation or prioritising of these reasons.

Candidates may provide a number of straightforward reasons, a smaller number of developed reasons, or a combination of these.

Up to the total mark allocation for this question: 1 mark should be given for each accurate relevant point. A second mark should be given for any mark that is developed.

Possible reasons may include:

- The First World War made worse pre-existing problems in Italy.

- Deep divisions between socialists and nationalists and liberals.

- Re-emergence of strike movement after the end of the war.

- Economic problems following the end of the war.

- Nationalist outrage and national disappointment at the perceived injustices of the Treaty of Versailles.

- Nationalists blamed this on the Liberal/Conservatives – D'Annunzio – takeover of Fiume in 1920.

- The Democratic constitution made it difficult to provide consistent policy.

- Any other relevant and accurate point of explanation.

Sources A and **B** are about Mussolini's domestic policies.

Source A

When Mussolini became Prime Minister in October 1922, he had to tackle the problems that had confronted the Italian state throughout its existence. In terms of domestic policy, it might be argued that Mussolini was more successful than his predecessors in one respect. By direct and ruthless political methods, he put an end to the divisions and in-fighting that had marked Italian politics throughout the previous century. His great talent, perhaps his only talent, was the acquisition and advertisement of power.

Source B

> Mussolini's declared policy was not of course simply to extend his own power. Against communist encouragement of class warfare as a means to a new society, he preached the need to unite all classes in service to the existing state. An upholder of private property and differences in wealth and status, he nevertheless believed that the welfare of the individual should be strictly subordinate to that of the nation. These ideas underlay the gradual development of what the Fascists called 'the corporate state'... Greater political stability, the fast increasing industrial prosperity and the beginning of a great new programme of public works helped to commend Mussolini whole-heartedly to the Italian people.

2. Compare the views of **Sources A** and **B** about Mussolini's domestic social and economic policies. (Compare the sources overall and/or in detail). **4**

Candidates can be credited in a number of ways up to a maximum of 4 marks.

Candidates must make direct comparisons between the two sources either overall or in detail. A simple comparison will indicate what points of detail or overall comparison they agree or disagree about and should be given 1 mark. A developed comparison in detail or overall viewpoint should be given 2 marks.

Candidates may achieve full marks by making four simple points, two developed points or a combination of these.

Possible points of comparison may include:

Source A	Source B
Overall Mussolini's achievements were limited and crudely executed and his popularity was based on fear and propaganda.	Overall Mussolini's declared, publicly stated policies were based on an ideology and won support from the people.
Mussolini's only talent was to gain and advertise power.	There was more to Mussolini's Fascism than just keeping him in power.
Mussolini used force to put an end to the in-fighting and divisions that had long existed in Italian society.	All classes had to unite to the service of the state.
Mussolini was more successful than his predecessors in domestic affairs but only in ending in-fighting.	Gradually Mussolini's policies commended him to the Italian people.

Source C is about the Abyssinian crisis of 1935-6.

Source C

> Encouraged no doubt by the ease with which Japan had got her way over Manchuria, Italy, which had long coveted the only large tract of Africa still ruled by Africans, in October 1935 invaded Abyssinia. Preparations had been going on for many months, and doubtless Mussolini thought that his friends the British and French were prepared to turn a blind eye. This time, however, the powers, partly impelled by public opinion, resolved to do something more than protest. The League invoked Article XVI and economic sanctions were quickly applied against Italy. But the policy was not wholeheartedly pressed... The French premier, Pierre Laval and the British Foreign Secretary, Sir Samuel Hoare, concocted a compromise scheme by which Italy would be allowed one large part of Abyssinia as an outright possession and another large part as a zone of economic expansion and development.

3. How fully does **Source C** explain the impact of the Abyssinian crisis on Italian Foreign Policy? (Use **Source C** and recall.)   **6**

Candidates must make an overall judgement about the extent to which the source provides a full description/explanation of a given event or development.

One mark will be given for each valid point interpreted from the source or each valid point of significant omission provided. The candidate can achieve up to 3 marks for their interpretation of the parts of the source they consider relevant in terms of the proposed question, where there is also at least one point of significant omission identified to imply a judgement has been made about the limitations of the source.

For full marks to be given each point needs to be discretely mentioned in terms of the question.

Possible points that may be mentioned from the source include:

*   The Manchurian crisis led Mussolini to believe that he could get away with an invasion designed to expand the Italian Empire.

*   Specifically, because he was allied to Britain and France, he believed that those two most powerful countries in particular would turn a blind eye.

*   Public opinion required that the League of Nations should take action.

*   Imposing economic sanctions did nothing to stop Mussolini as they were only imposed half-heartedly and Hoare and Laval tried to appease Italy

Possible points of omission include:

*   Mussolini felt let down by his allies in the Stresa Front, yet was not discouraged by the weak use of sanctions.

*   Encouraged by the supposed purifying impact of war on Italian manhood, Mussolini quickly became involved in the Spanish Civil War.

- With the end of the Stresa Front, Mussolini gradually grew closer to Hitler.

- Any other reasonable and relevant point.

4. Describe the means by which the Fascist government suppressed opposition to the government. **5**

Candidates must make a number of relevant, factual points. These should be key points. The points do not need to be in any particular order. The candidate may provide a number of straightforward points or a smaller number of developed points, or a combination of these.

Up to the total mark allocation for this question: 1 mark should be given for each accurate relevant point of knowledge. A second mark should be given for any point that is developed.

Candidates can be credited in a number of ways up to a maximum of 5 marks. They may take different perspectives on the events and may describe a variety of different aspects of the events.

Possible points of knowledge include:

- Unlike Hitler, Mussolini had to build his power over time.

- The murder of Giacomo Matteotti was a symbol of the Fascist use of thuggery and beatings to intimidate opposition, but brought criticism that initially in 1924 threatened Mussolini's position.

- The Acerbo Law gave the Fascists a permanent majority in parliament.

- The Aventine Protesters played into Mussolini's hands by walking out of Parliament.

- The King, Victor Emmanuel, gave Mussolini his backing because he distrusted the Republicanism of opposition politicians.

- The OVRA was a secret police force that had arrested and imprisoned over 4000 members of the opposition by 1940.

- The Lateran Treaties gave Mussolini access to the support of many Roman Catholics that might have otherwise opposed Fascism.

- Trade Unions that might have provided opposition to Fascism were incorporated into the Fascist Corporations.

- Parliament was abolished in 1939.

- Any other relevant and accurate point.

Part J – The Cold War, 1945–1989

Source A is about relations between America and the Soviet Union at the end of World War Two.

Source A

Despite contrasting ideologies, in 1945 the Cold War in Europe had not yet taken its final form. Although under Roosevelt and Truman there was growing suspicion, their inclination was to work with the Soviets and they were under pressure to disengage from European affairs. Stalin was not bent on unlimited expansion, however, and was content to allow British control over Greece. The Cold War took shape most of all over the treatment of Germany. While The USSR stripped resources from Eastern Germany, Stalin saw the American Marshall Plan as a fundamental threat to his strategy for securing the defence of the Soviet Union.

1. How fully does **Source A** explain the reasons for the development of the Cold War in Europe after 1945? (Use **Source A** and recall.) **6**

Candidates must make an overall judgement about the extent to which the source provides a full description/explanation of a given event or development.

One mark will be given for each valid point interpreted from the source or each valid point of significant omission provided. The candidate can achieve up to 3 marks for their interpretation of the parts of the source they consider relevant in terms of the proposed question, where there is also at least one point of significant omission identified to imply a judgement has been made about the limitations of the source.

For full marks to be given each point needs to be discretely mentioned in terms of the question.

Possible points that may be mentioned from the source include:

*   Ideological differences played a role, but were not the main reason.

*   Antagonism between Truman and Roosevelt on the one hand and Stalin on the other. Although he wanted to expand, Stalin was content for Britain to control Greece.

*   The most important area for conflict between the Soviet Union and the West was over Germany.

*   In particular Stalin saw the Marshall Plan's pumping of resources into Western Europe, in contrast to the Soviet policy of stripping Germany of resources, as an act of war, or at least as a fundamental threat to Soviet security.

Possible points of omission include:

*   The statement of the Truman Doctrine in 1947 – to resist communist takeovers anywhere in the world – centred around the fate of Turkey, not Germany.

- The 1948 attempted blockade of Berlin by the Soviet Union, and the US and British airlift that combatted it confirmed that the West would be prepared to go to the point of war to defend existing democratic states.

- This was followed by the establishment of NATO to secure US involvement in the defence of Western Europe in the long-term.

- Disagreements between Yalta and Potsdam, particularly regarding the atomic bomb, was a factor, but not the most important one.

Sources B and **C** are about the building of the Berlin Wall in 1961.

Source B

East Germany remained an artificial state and the appeal of its neighbour was enhanced by the accessibility of West German TV in most of the GDR. Denied true democracy, East Germans voted with their feet. In the 1950s the GDR was the only Soviet Bloc country to decline in population, from 19 million to 17 million, as people slipped through the unchecked exits into West Berlin and thence to the Federal Republic.

Faced with this haemorrhage of personnel, Ulbricht finally persuaded Moscow to seal off the city and begin the Berlin Wall on 13 August 1961.

Source C

In 1961 a new Soviet leader, Nikita Khrushchev, again felt confident enough to try to challenge the West over Berlin. He felt that the new US president, John Kennedy, was weak, as Khrushchev had scored a propaganda victory over the USA the previous year by shooting down an American U2 spy plane and publicly displaying its pilot, Gary Powers. By August 1961, 3000 refugees per day were pouring from impoverished East Berlin into West Berlin. Khrushchev tried to bully Kennedy into withdrawing from West Berlin. When this failed he ordered the building of a wall to cut West Berlin in two.

2. Compare the views of **Sources B** and **C** about the reasons for the building of the Berlin Wall. (Compare the sources overall and/or in detail). **4**

Candidates can be credited in a number of ways up to a maximum of 4 marks.

Candidates must make direct comparisons between the two sources either overall or in detail. A simple comparison will indicate what points of detail or overall comparison they agree or disagree about and should be given one mark.

A developed comparison in detail or overall viewpoint should be given 2 marks. Candidates may achieve full marks by making four simple points, two developed points or a combination of these.

Source A	Source B
Source A suggests that the initiative for the Wall came from the East German leader, Ulbricht	Source B suggests that the initiative for the Wall came from Khrushchev.
West Berlin TV showed the difference in living standards between West and East.	Khrushchev wanted to test Kennedy.
Hundreds of thousands of Berliners were 'voting with their feet', leaving East Berlin	3000 refugees per day going into West Berlin.
Ulbricht, worried about the loss of personnel, persuaded Khrushchev to build the wall.	Khrushchev hoped to bully Kennedy into leaving Berlin following his success over Gary Powers.

3. Explain the failure of American forces to defeat the Vietcong in the Vietnam War. **5**

Candidates must make a number of points that make the issue plain or clear, for example by showing connections between factors or causal relationships between ideas or events. These should be key reasons and may include theoretical ideas. There is no need for any evaluation or prioritising of these reasons.

Candidates may provide a number of straightforward reasons, a smaller number of developed reasons, or a combination of these.

Up to the total mark allocation for this question: 1 mark should be given for each accurate relevant point. A second mark should be given for any mark that is developed.

Possible reasons may include:

- US relied on state-of-the-art equipment, the Viet Cong (National Liberation Front) on improvised weapons such as home-made grenades and pits of poisoned spikes.

- Viet Cong tactics had a psychological impact on US troops.

- The Viet Cong used an elaborate system of tunnels and local knowledge to evade detection.

- The Ho Chi Minh Trail ensured a supply of trained recruits and supplies from the North.

- 300 000 volunteers by 1962.

- Tet Offensive, 1967, garnered considerable publicity in US media.

- The Anti-War movement in the USA reduced the American will to fight.

- The election of President Nixon and policy of Vietnamisation.

- Losses at Hamburger Hill and scandal of the Mai Lai massacre sealed American decision to withdraw.

4. Describe the development of the policy of Detente between the Superpowers in the 1970s and 1980s. **5**

Candidates must make a number of relevant, factual points. These should be key points. The points do not need to be in any particular order. The candidate may provide a number of straightforward points or a smaller number of developed points, or a combination of these.

Up to the total mark allocation for this question: 1 mark should be given for each accurate relevant point of knowledge. A second mark should be given for any point that is developed.

Candidates can be credited in a number of ways up to a maximum of 5 marks. They may take different perspectives on the events and may describe a variety of different aspects of the events.

Possible points of knowledge include:

- The arms race was a huge expense at a time of increasing economic difficulties, caused by the oil crisis (increasing price of oil) particularly.

- In the USA the protests against Vietnam and the growing CND movement in Britain and elsewhere created pressure to find alternative approaches to relations between East and West.

- The Cuban Missile Crisis had raised the possibility of a war starting 'by accident' and had led to the setting up of the 'Hotline' between Moscow and Washington.

- Nixon hoped to exploit differences between China and Russia by building relations with China.

- Nixon visited Moscow, Brezhnev visited Washington.

- Amongst the early achievements of Detente were the 1968 Nuclear Non-proliferation Treaty, the 1971 US Table Tennis tour of China, Nixon's visit to China, US withdrawing her veto to Communist China joining the UN.

- SALT 1, The Helsinki Agreement and the meeting in space between US and Soviet spacecraft sought to improve relations between the US and the Soviet Union.

- Much of the detente of the 1970s was symbolic and did not make a great difference in practice.

- Detente ended after 1979, beginning with the Soviet invasion of Afghanistan and growing Soviet influence in developing countries.

- Ronald Reagan became President, declaring the Soviet Union to be an 'Evil Empire'.

- Detente re-emerged with the rise of Mikhail Gorbachev as leader of the Soviet Union in 1985.

- Gorbachev permitted the relaxation of Soviet control in Eastern Europe.

- The Berlin Wall was dismantled in 1989.